D0815564

How
To
Be
Loved

How To Be Loved

W. W. Broadbent, M.D.

PRENTICE-HALL, INC.

Englewood Cliffs

N.J.

How to Be Loved by W.W. Broadbent, M.D.

Printed in the United States of America

Prentice-Hall International, Inc., London
Prentice-Hall of Australia, Pty. Ltd., Sydney
Prentice-Hall of Canada, Ltd., Toronto
Prentice-Hall of India Private Ltd., New Delhi
Prentice-Hall of Japan, Inc., Tokyo

10 9 8 7 6 5 4 3 2 1

Library of Congress Cataloging in Publication Data

Broadbent, W W
    How to be loved.

    Bibliography: P.
    Includes index.
    1. Love.   I. Title.
BF575.L8B73   158′.1   75-38589
ISBN 0-13-402149-5

TO
MARK *and* MELODY *and* STEVE
and to
LILL;
who taught me how to
love and be loved

This is a most unusual book for a psychiatrist to write. It is simple, down-to-earth, and full of gentle wisdom. Dr. Broadbent's aim is to help individuals to own themselves —feelings, thoughts, behavior—in a friendly way. He gives various helpful examples of checking-in to discover what one's own reactions are; and other ways of checking-out with others to learn what they are actually feeling, rather than what we think they are feeling.

Dr. Broadbent has a personal and winning way of enabling the reader to put these ways of being into action for himself. In my judgment, the book could have only a helpful effect on any reader.

CARL R. ROGERS
Resident Fellow
Center for Studies of the Person

AUTHOR'S NOTE

I believe the brain is the only thing that ever tried to analyze itself. This, alone, is difficult to do, but when the brain puts itself to the task of analyzing someone else's brain, things get complicated. Psychiatry can attest to this. It's not my intention to analyze brains as much as to take inventory of what is happening and describe what I see. It would be stretching a point to regard this book as scientific or even psychiatric in the strict sense of those words. As much as possible, I have deliberately used language which is neither psychiatric nor scientific. In fact, any similarity between what you read and what is called "the scientific method" or "analytic method" is unintended and purely coincidental.

The dialogues herein, except for three, are taken from either video or audio tape playbacks—the three exceptions are taken from notes or memory. In these dialogues, for the most part, I deal with the "how" not the "why" of the communication, i.e. I attend to the form or style of the communicator as opposed to the substance of the conversation itself. The observations are made in the here and now and are of a low order of inference. There is no serious attempt to achieve insight, that is, to connect the past with the present. It's hard enough for me to connect the present —to just listen to and look at the torrent of messages that accompany a trickle of words in the present moment. Sometimes, there are so many messages I don't know where to begin. But on reflection, when I remind myself that everyone wants to belong, I begin with how he is belonging with me.

W. W. BROADBENT

ACKNOWLEDGMENTS

*I believe that some people may be born "mind bumpers."
It is as though they have a special talent for jostling,
pushing, and pulling other people's minds into thinking
as they never thought before. My special mind bumpers,
those to whom I feel most indebted for my peculiar
thinking in the psychiatric field, include Franz Alexander,
Viktor E. Frankl, Helmuth Kaiser, Keery Merwin,
Fritz Perls, and Carl Rogers.*

*I am appreciative to Don Shepard, publishing agent in
Hollywood, and Gene Permé, associate editor for Prentice-
Hall. Their know-how and guidance were invaluable in
the publishing of the book. Gene flew from his office in
New Jersey to stay four days at our place in Long Beach,
California. He participated in group sessions plus a
workshop at my training center and worked day and night
with Lill and me in putting the final draft together.*

*In the preparation of the book, from its inception, I am
particularly grateful to my good friend and classmate
Brian Bull. Despite his demanding chores as chairman of
the Pathology Department at Loma Linda Medical
School, he has given countless hours of his time in the
multi-editing of the book, unstintingly offering his
unsolicited insults of my alleged writing ability—a labor
of love if there ever was one.*

The book is a product of daily, ongoing conferences I had with my wife, Lill. I don't know how to measure her contribution, both in form and in content. How do you measure gentleness and love? I'll appreciate it if you bear in mind that whatever you read from here on, our responsibility for it is as one.

CONTENTS

1

Everyone
Wants
to
Belong

IMAGINE YOURSELF THE ONLY PERSON WHO
ever lived—no one before you, no one with you, no
animals, just you—with all your food, water, and
climatic needs satisfied. In this fantasy try to shut out as
much of the external environment as possible. Find a
quiet spot, close your eyes, and try to imagine the kind of
feelings, any feelings, you would have in this world
without people. You can picture yourself on a beautiful,
lush, subtropical island if you wish, but remember, you
have *never* seen or heard another human being. Don't
read past this paragraph for a moment or two. Just close
your eyes and fantasize how you would feel.

As you are now aware, you couldn't feel envious of anyone. You couldn't feel inferior or superior, self-conscious, embarrassed, or suspicious. You couldn't even feel lonely because you'd have no basis for comparison. You have to experience something in order to miss it. Even feeling self-respect would be difficult. For example, you'd have no dishonest person against whom to measure your honesty. You couldn't experience anger, love, hate, or frustration toward anyone because many, if not most, of your psychological feelings are related to people. The kinds of feelings you experience have much to do with how people relate to you. And how people relate to you has much to do with how you relate to people—how you communicate with them.

What this boils down to is that if it weren't for people, you wouldn't have many problems. You wouldn't have much happiness either, but at least you wouldn't have as many problems. The point is that how content or discontent you are is largely dependent on how *you* actually belong with others—that is, the extent to which you are accepted, approved, and loved.

Everyone wants to belong, but many just don't know how to go about it. The hard fact is that some of us seem to experience much belonging and others very little. Some of us are very accepted by most people, and others aren't. Some seem to find an ongoing permanent love, and others stumble out of one alleged love experience into another.

In a world that talks and sings so much about love, why is there so little of it?

Here are some actual statements various individuals have made to me while in session:

"I don't believe anyone, not even Joe or the children, really cares for me. But I couldn't make it on my own financially. I feel trapped."

"I don't love him and he doesn't love me. We tolerate each other, but I can't stand being alone. So it's better than nothing."

"While I'm talking I feel that what I'm saying is unimportant and that people would like to get away from me."

"It seems that when I'm involved with a man I have something, and for a while I'm happy. Then, when we fall out, I'm down again. No, I don't have what you'd call a real friend."

"Oh, I know lots of people and I'm nice to them. But they're just interested in themselves. I know they aren't interested in me."

"Yes, I live alone. It's easier that way. I haven't met anyone yet who really accepts me as I am."

"I don't think I'm capable of loving anyone anymore. I've been taken advantage of so many times."

"If the children were older, I'm sure we'd get a divorce."

Eleven-year-old: "Nobody likes me." (Therapist: I like

you.") "But you don't live with me twenty-four hours a day."

The general psychiatric solution to the dilemma of the unloved is to encourage them to gain insight—that is, to connect the past with the present in order to understand *why* they do what they do. Sadly, this 20-20 hindsight hasn't resulted in very many cures for being unloved. The new psychological growth centers that have sprung up teach many of their devotees how to play authentic and autonomous but give few answers on how to be loved. The solutions offered by philosophers on earth and philosophers who claim to have transcended this earth seem to leave as many unloved souls as ever.

In looking for an explanation, I wanted the following question answered: "Is there a *common principle* of behavior that is *lacking* in the unloved that results in their not experiencing a real sense of belonging?" I initially focused only on those who were unloved to find the common factor missing in their behavior that fostered their being unloved. Trying to find something that isn't there is difficult. Whereas previously I was merely confused, at least now I was efficiently organizing my confusion. I discovered some who were introverted and others who were extroverted, some who were assertive and others who were unassertive, some who were empathic and others who were not, and some who were pretty and some who were plain. One individual was unusually seductive and attracted men like bees to honey but felt unloved—and, in fact, was not loved by men. She was convenient for them. I could find no *common* factor *missing* in their collective behavior that could explain their being so poorly loved.

Not finding a missing factor in the unloved, I focused attention on those who were loved, this time looking for a common factor *present* in their behavior. Again I found people who were extroverted and introverted, assertive and unassertive, empathic and unempathic, pretty and plain. And still a common principle of behavior eluded me. There was more honesty in some, more givingness in others, more unselfishness and other positive qualities in still others. But there was no one single principle—no something extra that the loved possessed that the unloved didn't.

While I couldn't find this certain extra something the loved ones *had,* I did find a common something the loved ones *did not have.* In the loved I found very few habits of manipulating others in order to be accepted. And when I focused again on the unloved, I found an almost limitless array of communicative habits that, like an incessant Morse code, were constantly sending the extra message: "Approve of me. Accept me. Respect me. Love me." Whether the communication lasted a few seconds or a few minutes, whether verbal or nonverbal, there was this quietly desperate attempt to stir others to view them favorably. This was the underlying common principle in the behavior of the unloved. Each of the unloved, in his own *habitual* way, was constantly absorbed in the practice of sending extra messages through his words or intonations or facial expressions or body movements with the common design of being approved by one and all.

The following schematics demonstrate this process:

HABITS

boisterous
raucous
dirty stories
glad hand
JOHN + *slap on the back* = *Seeking*
big smile   *approval, acceptance,*
                  love from others.
life of the party
knows it all
sensationalist

HABITS
quiet
modest
unassertive
passive
deferring   *Seeking*
TOM + *speaks only when* = *approval, acceptance,*
   spoken to   *love from others.*
superpolite
minimal body
  movement
talks in general
  terms

6

MARY + *HABITS*
theatrical
coy
seductive
flighty
talkative
naïve
animated
provocatively
  dressed
emotional
= *Seeking*
approval, acceptance,
love from others.

JOAN + *HABITS*
intellectual
chatterer
fashionable
interminably
  sweet
prestige-
  conscious
talks about her
  voyages
lives in a world
  of "shoulds"
= *Seeking*
approval, acceptance,
love from others.

DICK + *HABITS*
multi-complaints
indecisive
hypersensitive
inner-directed
"Life is a burden
  to me."
"See how I smile
  through it all."
advice-seeking
= *Seeking*
approval, acceptance,
love from others.

These habits *do* work at times in arousing acceptance, at least ostensibly. As long as there are manipulators there'll be manipulatees. However, the degree of belonging—that is, of being loved or accepted—that a person experiences in this way is minimal and less than fulfilling. I believe the reason for this is that whenever someone is striving to look good, trying to exhort others to accept or love him, others generally sense what he's doing, either consciously or unconsciously, and are not drawn to him.

In daily life, whenever John, Tom, Mary, Joan, or Dick sense that they're not being approved or accepted, something curious happens. Despite the fact that raucousness, nonassertiveness, theatrical behavior, chattering, or complaining often tend to produce the opposite of approval, John becomes more raucous, Tom more unassertive, Mary more theatrical, Joan more of a chatterer, and Dick more complaining. Each pours copious energies into the effort of *trying to belong,** each doing the best he can with the tools he has to work with. They just don't know any other way.

I would like to make clear that the examples shown do not refer to *occasional* behavior such as appropriate smiling or telling a joke once in a while. The reference here is to the *ongoing, constant, inordinate habits that make up a style of behavior.*

---

* *Trying to belong,* as used in this book, means unconscious manipulation of others in order to belong. Implicit in the verb *trying* are the ideas of entreating, exhorting, coercing, exploiting, enticing, appealing, persuading, demanding, and complying.

The picture of trying to be loved has many hues and colors, many forms and styles. The accident-prone boy habitually "cries" for you to love him. The compliant girl is habitually "good" for you to love her. The rebellious girl may habitually "test" your love for her. The dominating husband habitually "demands" that you love him, and the subservient wife habitually "complies" that you love her.

Consider an interaction between a dominating man and his habitually subservient wife:

FATHER: *Well, I see you finally mowed the lawn.*

SON: *Yeah, I did it before you came home.*

FATHER: (Demeaning tone) *Well, there's plenty to do yet. The walk has to be swept, and you're just sitting there reading the paper.*

SON: *I was just resting after dinner. I'll be getting on it after a few minutes. Mom called me in to dinner before I'd finished.*

FATHER: *Yeah, that's what you say. I'll bet if I hadn't said anything, you'd just let it go.*

MOTHER: (Plaintive tone) *John, I did call him to dinner before he'd finished.*

FATHER: (Raised voice, commanding tone) *Now you keep the hell out of this. This is between me and him. You take care of your dishes, and I'll take care of him.*

MOTHER: (Plaintive tone) *I was only trying to help.*

FATHER: (Yelling) *You're not helping. You're hindering. Now keep out of it.*

SON: (Puts paper down and goes out to sweep walk)

The dominant person is not necessarily a leader, since a leader needs a cause. All the dominant person needs is someone to dominate. The subservient person is not necessarily a follower, since a follower also needs a cause. All the subservient one needs is to be dominated, and thus they belong to each other—like a lion and a lamb, one being absorbed by the other.

Both want to belong, but they have acquired habits of communicating that sabotage real belonging. Each employs habits that involve trying to be loved, one demanding for it, the other complying for it. Belonging, in this sense, is more accurately termed *quasi-belonging* or fusion by delusion.

The basic assumption here is that the essence of belonging or being loved is not to try to manipulate others for it—not to seduce for it, demand, cajole, grovel, nor pout for it. I want to make clear that "not trying" to be loved does not mean "Take me as I am." Nor does it mean one is not to put forth effort in being fair to enhance a relationship for the sake of the relationship. Above all, "not trying to be loved" in no way suggests that you not try to make another happy. On the contrary, trying to bring pleasure to someone because of the pleasure you feel in that person's pleasure is perhaps the most beautiful demonstration of love known.

This is quite different from habitually trying to make someone happy by flattery, sycophancy, buffoonery, servility, or such in order to get him to love you. This kind of manipulation is a form of barter. You are trying to buy the person's love for you, and this is often resented. The essence of being loved, therefore, is peeling off the "trying" habits, the *quasi-belonging* habits, like barnacles off a ship, revealing the beauty that has always been there.

Stated simply, it becomes: "One of the secrets of being loved is not to try to be loved."

2
Quasi -
Belonging
Styles

Before illustrating what I call quasi-
belonging styles, I want to briefly clarify the difference
between *quasi-belonging* and *actual-belonging*. It's a
difficult chore, since there is really no clear-cut boundary
line between the two.

Actual-belonging, in its purest sense, is manifested
when two people experience a sense of well-being
together without covertly trying to manipulate each
other for acceptance, approval, or love. There is no
inordinate entertaining, being sexy, being manly, servile,
intellectual, naïve, saintly, or other style used to extract
one's pound of belonging from another. To *actual-belong*

means respecting the feelings and separateness of the other. Implicit in this is that one may choose to divert or postpone his immediate wishes in deference to the other without absorbing or being absorbed by the other.

Quasi-belonging is a simulated belonging, like a shadow or an echo of the real thing. It is experienced through the sacrifice of one's integrity and unique identity. This form of belonging is characterized by ambiguity. A continuous torrent of double messages, one verbal, the other nonverbal, seeks to deluge others to view him favorably. *Quasi-belonging* is a learned process. When you come down the birth canal, you're an actual-belonger. You don't pop out with, "How do you do, Doctor? You certainly did an outstanding job of delivering me. I'm going to recommend you to the chairman of the Obstetrics Department. And I want to take this opportunity to thank my mother and father, who made all this possible." It isn't until after you're born that flattery is learned as one of the many levers for trying to move others to accept you. Rather, when you come down the birth canal, you are totally authentic, honest, and congruent (what you experience outside, what you feel inside, and what you utter to the world all go down the same track at the same time), and you communicate, "What the hell is the idea of taking me out of that idyllic, warm, peaceful atmosphere and dumping me into this gravity-dominated, hard, smelly, blinding environment, where I even have to breathe on my own?" You may not use these exact words, but you get the idea across to the obstetrician.

An illustration of quasi-belonging is the *ritual of modesty*. There are three rules to be followed:

1. Never admit to anyone how adequate you really believe you are nor the degree of esteem you may feel for yourself.

2. Always underplay any complimentary remarks directed toward yourself.

   JOE: *You played that Beethoven Sonata with such feelings. It was beautiful.*

   TOM: *Oh, gosh, I'm no Horowitz or Rubinstein. I really just play at the piano.*

   JOE: *Oh, you're too modest.*

   TOM: *Thank you.*

3. If necessary, lie.

   JOE: *You scored forty of the sixty points in that basketball game. You were outstanding.*

   TOM: *Aw, I was lucky.*

Both the sender and the receiver of the "modest" message may be aware of what is going on, of the ceremonious nature of the role each is playing. That which is usually out of awareness is the extra *nonverbal* message of the interaction. Each is co-operating with the other in the socially sanctioned ritual of a mutual psychological message. The goal is to reduce the tension that results from being a totally honest, separate individual by nonverbally creating an illusion of belonging with another in a heap of humbleness, thus blunting awareness of one's own identity, one's own genuine feelings. An example of actual-belonging would be:

JOE: *You played that sonata beautifully.*

TOM: *Thank you. I appreciate that.*

Another quasi-belonging process is the *howdy-do ritual:*

TOM: *Hello, Joe. How's it going?*

JOE: *Oh, not bad. What's with you?*

TOM: *Nothing much. Same old thing.*

JOE: *How's old Frank doing nowadays?*

TOM: *Frank died last year. He was—*

JOE: *Yeah, Frank's a great ole boy. Say hello to him for me next time you see him.*

TOM: *Uh, well, I—*

JOE: *Gotta run now. See you around, Tom.*

TOM: *Uh, yeah—okay, Joe. See you later.*

I believe that most recognize the *howdy-do ritual* as a ritual and realize that sometimes neither party is really listening to the other. Still, even in this exaggerated dialogue, there is some physical awareness that is mutually affirming: "I'm a human being. You're a human being. We're existing in this world together, and we acknowledge each other." Even in this brief meeting there is, at least, a sense of simulated belonging, though the belonging experience is minimal.

The experience of human belonging is activated whenever two or more entities are together. This can happen between a person and his God, a person and nature, a person and his native land, a person and another person, or a person and his dog. At this time, I'm restricting the meaning of "belonging" to that which evolves whenever two or more people are together, *no matter what the relationship is.* Belonging doesn't happen now and then. It's an ongoing, *moment-to-moment* process. How fulfilling any belonging experience may be is directly proportional to the minimization of the impulse to strive, try, ritualize, or manipulate for approval or love. The less one tries to manipulate for acceptance, the more he is accepted. Thus, one of the secrets for looking good is not to try to look good.

The communication system used in quasi-belonging fluctuates. It can be indirect or vague or hinting, nonlistening, unauthentic, support-seeking, demanding, persuading, responsibility-reducing, fencing, unassertive, but above all, it is *ambiguous. Two dissimilar messages are being sent simultaneously—one verbal, the other nonverbal.* The following quasi-belonging styles demonstrate this enigmatic process of communicating double messages. While my personality interjects occasional humor into what I'm writing, it's not with the intent of ridiculing a human being. I would like one to laugh at a particular fragment of his personality with me. I believe with Gordon Allport and Viktor Frankl that when one can truly laugh at his so-called neurosis, it ceases to be fed and tends to melt away.

MAN'S-MAN STYLE

The prototype for the Man's-Man Style is the Hollywood "he-man." It describes someone who is suffering from a case of terminal masculinity. Ed manifests his he-manhood by his well-timed snickers, his challenging gaze, and his general nonverbal habits which communicate, "I'm absolutely fearless."

TOM: *When you laugh like that while I'm talking, it's like you're putting me down.*

ED: *So?*

TOM: *Well, I don't like it.*

ED: (Snickers) *So?*

DR. B.: *Ed, will you give the snicker a voice? What is the extra message of the snicker?*

ED: (Snickers again) *It means—oh, I don't know what it means. Maybe it means, "So what does he want— for me to hold his hand?"*

DR. B.: *Would you say you are putting Tom down right now?*

ED: *He's already down.*

DR. B.: *Who's up?*

ED: *I don't know—me, I guess.*

DR. B.: *Ed, are you afraid of not being up, on top of others? Is that what you're afraid of?*

ED: (Gives Dr. B. long, derisive look)

DR. B.: *You're looking at me awfully hard, Ed. Would you feel more comfortable if I were afraid of you?*

ED: (Turning his gaze away from Dr. B., smiling as though his hand is caught in the cookie jar)

DR. B.: *Give your smile a voice. What is your smile saying?*

ED: *My smile?*

DR. B.: *Yes. How aware are you of yourself? Check-in. What is your smile saying? Are you happy?*

ED: *Well, no, I'm not happy. I'm—my smile is saying —well, I'm mixed up.* (No smiling or snickering, most thoughtful, almost pensive gaze).

DR. B.: *Thank you.*

ED: *For what?*

DR. B.: *I appreciate your being honest with me.*

ED: (Smiling, glancing at Dr. B.) *Oh!*

DR. B.: *Ed, will you give the smile a voice now? Do you feel something now?*

ED: *Well, yeah. I liked what you said about me being honest. I feel a little happy, I suppose.*

DR. B.: *That's what I sensed, too. This time your smile and your feelings were on the same wave length. That's called congruency. It's a more genuine expression of yourself.*

The characteristics of this style involve direct, almost disdainful, occasionally squinting eye contact, a heavy gait, a minimum of body and facial movement, little smiling, and absolutely no crying. Vocal intonations and inflections manifest an absolute irreversible masculine virility. Physical contact with another man is limited to a hand crunch, a slap on the back, or a fist in the face. The overt and covert quasi-belonging message is: "I do not want you to have even the slightest doubt about my manhood. As you can see, I have no doubts. I'm really a man—really I am. In fact, I sneer at homosexuals. Especially I want you to know—all of you—that I'm not now, nor ever have been, nor ever will be afraid of you, and that means you and you and you. Now, just stand in line and extend your admiration, respect, and esteem for me—a real man! But if you can't give me anything else, at least, please, be somewhat afraid of me."

The inordinate behavior of this quasi-belonging style can be an overcompensation for self-doubts about one's manhood. It is a learned habit with strong cultural reinforcement (especially via movies and TV). It's possible that if a man's lib movement were instigated, freeing men from the many outcroppings of this style, there would be little need for women's lib. With sufficient desire one can unlearn this habit and relearn that a man is never a man until he's a gentle man. He can also learn that respect can come to him from others without his being feared by others.

SAINT STYLE

The Saint Style is characterized by an ecclesiastical sweetness, a benign countenance, a chronic saccharine smile, with the head often compassionately tilting to one side. The covert message is: "Can't you see my halo of mercy, how accepting, how understanding, not to mention how sweet I am? Can't you feel my immaculate reception of you? How could you reject anyone as obviously loving and unjudgmental as this? Come commiserate with me. Quasi-belong with me."

As with any compensatory mechanism, the "saint" may be hiding a devilish anger or judgmentalness totally beyond his own awareness. A person who has learned this style frequently attaches to others who adulate him. Generally these attachments are brief, since it takes a lot of energy to be saintly for very long.

WINDY STYLE

The individual with the Windy Style rarely takes the opportunity to say nothing when he has nothing to say, and dilutes his ideas with a Niagara Falls of words. He is often so infatuated with his words that it seems he hates to give up the ideas that might be associated with them. He assumes others similarly admire his endless verbiage. Beyond his awareness may be the fear of possible rejection through an undiluted human-to-human contact. His words may be serving the function of porcupine quills keeping people at a distance. The extra message: "Admire, respect, and accept my articulation, but don't get too close lest you really see me and run away."

CHAMELEON STYLE

Mary practices the Chameleon Style by trying to find out what is expected of her and then complying in order to be accepted.

JOE: *Mary, how do you feel inside when Bill [Dr. B.] teases you about how compliant you are, how you have the habit of not saying how you really feel?*

MARY: (Evading the question) *Well, he's right, I do do that.*

JOE: *I mean I don't know how you feel about it. Do you feel embarrassed or angry when he says that?*

MARY: (Not responding to the question) *I feel he's right, and I need someone to tell me I don't let people know where I am. [Extra message: If I owned my feelings, like embarrassment, anger, or whatever, then you might disapprove of me.]*

HELEN: *I don't believe you're like that though, are you?*

MARY: (Compliant) *Well, no. Sometimes I'm not.*

DR. B.: *You aren't?*

MARY: (Compliant) *Well, I guess I am.* (Mary and the whole group laugh when they realize she is contradicting herself in trying to meet with both Helen's and Bill's expectations.)

MARY: *The fact is I do have my own thoughts and feelings.* (Group applauds) *And the fact is I'm not always compliant and I feel frightened saying all this.* (Much affirmation from group)

The individual who employs the Chameleon Style waits and watches, assessing the likes, dislikes, and value system of whomever he contacts. Once he divines what is expected of him, he sacrifices his own identity and is frequently absorbed into the personality of the other. The extra quasi-belonging message is: "I'm whatever you want me to be. You're a car talker? Then I'm a car talker. Religion is important? Then religion is important. Religion is unimportant? Then religion is unimportant. I have a ticket of admission to whatever show you want me to put on. Now then, I dare you to try to disapprove of me. I've virtually stripped myself of my identity for you." This style usually quasi-belongs best with the style that must always be right.

MORALIZER STYLE

"All my thoughts are virtuous, patriotic, and righteous, and I want you all to know it." The extra message: "If my wonderful goodness will not inspire your awe of me, then shame on you." The individual who has adopted this style lives in a world of "shoulds," continually rehearsing for his next social role.

FRIGHTENED-FAWN-IN-THE-FOREST STYLE

This individual, usually a woman, denies her individuality and wholeness by habitually sending a message that she is weak, delicate, defenseless, frightened, and in need of protection. The unconscious design is to tether herself to a protector, a supporter— anyone who will veil the fawn's awareness of her unique self and assume the responsibility for her words and deeds. The extra nonverbal message is: "Please approach me gently, softly, as though you are walking through the forest in moccasins. Tread carefully and quietly, lest the slightest discordant sound shatter me." This individual tends to quasi-belong with those who respond with a super-self-sufficient fathering leash.

SUPER-SELF-SUFFICIENT STYLE OR HOLIER-THAN-THOU STYLE

The antithesis of the Frightened Fawn in the Forest Style is the Super-Self-sufficient Style. The quasi-belonging edict here is: "I don't need you. I don't need him. I don't need anyone. I don't care what you say to me because I'm above all that. Now then, don't you admire, respect, look up to, and want to belong with someone who is so well able to take care of himself and who needs nothing from you?" A frequent physical concomitant of this style is the raised brow and slightly elevated chin. Oftentimes imperious behavior such as this is a compensatory posture. The individual's habitation to presenting himself as super-self-sufficient may arise out of his fears of rejection or his repressed feelings of inferiority. Actually he is not inferior but assumes others may see him as such. He usually mates with the Frightened Fawn in the Forest who is no threat to him or with a particularly accepting woman who indulges him—at least for a while.

MARTYR STYLE

"Oh, what I've done for you and what do I get in return? Absolutely nothing." (Usually holds hand over chest during this verbiage and rarely enjoys the luxury of suffering in private.) The extra message: "See the depth of my misery, the crown of thorns that I bear. Feel guilty, give me sympathy, and do what the hell I want you to do, goddamm it." (Face often portrays woebegone torment.) Some parents are virtuosos in this style. I suspect they learned it from their parents and now are teaching it to their children, who may use it on their children. Quasi-belongs best with those who can carry loads of guilt and repressed resentment for the parent.

These quasi-belonging styles are seemingly unlimited in their variety. If you visit a football game and look around, you'll see a sea of unrepeated faces. Behind each face there's an unrepeated value system (a sense of what comes first, second, third, and so forth) and an unrepeated way of feeling and communicating—which together make up a style of belonging. But no matter by what name the style may be known, whether Windy or Chameleon, the silent plea is always the same: "Please accept me." And as funny as any single style may appear on paper with its ambiguity exposed, it isn't funny to the one who has acquired it. He may sense at times that he is not belonging as well as he'd like, but he doesn't entirely know what he's doing to create that situation.

He doesn't want you to regard him unfavorably, and he certainly doesn't seek your rejection, but it's the only style of belonging he knows. Thus, he's like the hamster in the treadmill. He goes round and round never quite reaching the other person in the fulfilling experience of belonging that he so desperately seeks.

Following are a few more of these quasi-belonging styles:

SEDUCTIVE STYLE

The Seductive Style is one of the most widely practiced
ceremonies of quasi-belonging and is usually an
outgrowth of love deprivation in childhood. We all need
love for breakfast, lunch, and dinner, and if we don't get
enough for breakfast and lunch early in life, we need
more for dinner later in life. The seduction process is,
for the most part, nonverbal. Though practiced by both
men and women, it is generally a culturally sanctioned
form of quasi-belonging for the latter. The long, lingering
look, the ambiguous innuendo, the come-hither glance,
the provocative dress, the touching, the pelvic dancing,
the soft voice—all are covertly saying, "I'm available. I'm
yours for the taking. I'm an easy lay." The tragic aspect
of this quasi-belonging ceremony is that the woman who
adopts this style does not usually have sexual intercourse
as her primary objective. Her lure is really designed for
attention without intention. She just wants to be
accepted, to be liked and admired as someone desirable.
The extent of her sexual desire may be to be cuddled,
something her father and mother could have done for
her earlier had they been psychologically healthier.
Another element of this behavior is the feeling of power
the seducer experiences over the seduced. Thus, those in
prestigious positions are often selected by the seducer so
that, at least in fantasy, the prestige of the seduced can
be shared, and for those fleeting moments the seducer
can palliate her feelings of worthlessness.

PLAYING-AUTHENTIC STYLE

"Look at the genuineness that floods my face. Listen to my pitiless honesty, my fearless epithets. Notice how direct I am. I say what I want, when I want, and to whom I want. I take pride in my rudeness." (Often suffering from severe groupiness of the think tank secondary to overexposure to alleged group therapy.) The philosophical base is: "Life is what you fake it." The extra message is: "My thing is authenticity. Admire and respect my authenticity. Therefore admire and respect me."

TOILET-BOWL SYNDROME

I've named this style the Toilet Bowl Syndrome because it's as though its practitioner is holding a toilet bowl over his head and saying, "Just look how the world is shitting on me." Helen employs the Toilet Bowl Syndrome:

HELEN: (Glazed eyes, furrowed brow, staring at the floor in a melancholy manner)

MARY: *You look depressed, Helen. Is it your children again?*

HELEN: (Sigh) *No, it's just that I don't think I'll ever be able to be close to anyone again. I've been walked on so much.*

MARY: *Did your boyfriend walk out on you?*

HELEN: *No. But we just sit around the house. We never go anywhere. We just watch TV.*

MARY: *Why don't you suggest to him that you go out? Wouldn't he take you out?*

27

HELEN: *Oh, he's taken me out, but I can't afford a baby-sitter.*

MARY: *Why don't you take the kids along?*

HELEN: *I need some adult conversation. All I ever hear is kids' problems and fighting.*

MARY: *How about your mother? Won't she baby-sit?*

HELEN: *Well, she has, but then I have to listen to her complaining about not feeling well or something.*

The subterranean fusing message is: "Woe is me. No matter where I turn or what I do, everything turns out wrong. Nothing turns out right. Now, don't you feel sorry and see how much I need your help?"

RED-CROSS-NURSE STYLE

The Red Cross Nurse Style is characterized by interminable supporting, reassuring, helping, advising, and counseling others, often to the exclusion of his or her family. The covert message is: "Can't you see how giving I am, how supportive I am, how I put myself out for you? Tell me your problem—no matter how intimate —I'm your supporter. If you doubt your manhood, I'm your athletic supporter. Even if I haven't the slightest idea what your real problem is, I have a bagful of solutions. Now, don't you feel obliged to accept me as the super-helper that I am?" The Toilet Bowl Syndrome acts like a magnet to the Red Cross Nurse, but only temporarily. Both styles need many individuals on whom to ply their respective bonding habits. In a short time the Red Cross Nurse is content to be flushed out of the Toilet Bowl's incessant stream of woe.

It must be remembered that the description of all these styles refers to inordinate, excessive habitual behavior only, with the unconscious design of achieving a sense of attachment with another.

GURU STYLE

The Guru Style person looks wisely, talks wisely, acts wisely, and occasionally even thinks wisely. He usually possesses a narrow knowledge of a broad sphere of data or a broad knowledge of a narrow sphere of data. Serves a full breast of abstruse advice and sage sayings with a profound dressing and a sprinkling of sense. The extra message: "Respect and admire my wiseness. Therefore, respect and admire me. Usually quasi-belongs with sycophants or lost souls seeking the answers to life.

ONE-UPSMAN STYLE

This person is habituated to one-upping—that is, to demonstrating that his mind is quicker and better than someone else's by trying to make someone appear ridiculous. The name of the contest is: "Always get in the last word." The extra message: "Attend to my facile scintillating tongue. My whole foundation of esteem is built on showing you the ingenuity and adroitness of my mind. Admire my artfulness and clever contrivances as I put someone down. Admire me." The unfortunate feature of this style is that while many are repelled by the cruelness of someone trying to gain esteem at the expense of others, there are often a few who will chuckle in amusement when someone is "one-upped"—and thus the style is reinforced.

FAN STYLE

"You're just great. Whatever you did, it was great." The person with the fan style can often be seen stomping his feet, holding his sides, and in general convulsing himself over some limp banter. He frequently pours piles of syrupy praise on some individual while in the presence of others. The extra message is: "There's no possible way you can escape loving me. I've trapped you in my fusillade of accolades."

PING-PONG STYLE

The individual with the Ping-Pong Style makes contact with others through the medium of bickering as though he is involved in a friendly Ping-Pong game. I use the term "friendly" because, while there is a competitive quality to the style, there is no overt animosity manifested. You can notice two features to this style: (1) the alertness of the practitioner to the weak link in the chain of thought of the other and (2) the frequent use of "yes, but" in the communication system.

BILL: *I really love this tennis. It's a great exercise, especially at my age.*

SAM: *Yes, but it's not a full exercise. You only use one arm all the time.*

BILL: *Well, I think it's better than none at all. We can all benefit from some kind of exercise.*

SAM: *Yes, but you can die from it, too, if you overdo it.*

BILL: *Oh, Sam, I'm talking about intelligently planned exercise. I believe we'll all live longer and better and think more clearly, too, if we took better care of ourselves.*

SAM: *My grandmother lived until she was eighty-five and she didn't exercise.*

BILL: *Are you saying you don't believe we should exercise?*

SAM: *Oh, no. It's just that I like to look at all sides of the question.*

The quasi-belonging process here is: "Let us belong via a contest of ideas. When you accept my friendly challenge, I can translate this into your acceptance of me." Unfortunately, the contentious one using this style does not endear himself to many people. He generally attracts those who are also fearful of close contact.

NICE-GUY STYLE

The overt communication of the person with this style is: "I always have the same nice face, same smile, and same charming manner no matter what you say or do." His covert communication is: "How could you help liking someone as friendly and unthreatening as a nice guy like me?" Unfortunately, the "nice guy" is often not so nice within the confines of his own home, for many of his suppressed and repressed feelings are vented on himself or his family.

SUPEROPINIONATED STYLE

The Superopinionator is usually of above-average intelligence, often well-read, and is generally a black-and-white thinker. He suffers from what I refer to as an *interferiority complex,* meaning he thrusts his opinions into dialogues without invitation, a conversation crasher. He can hardly wait until someone else is finished talking (and usually doesn't) so that he can make his point. His precept is: "Don't talk while I'm interrupting you." Not to be confused with the Guru. The latter, if he doesn't have knowledge of the subject, will remain in silent, bemused contemplation as though he knows all about it anyway. The Superopinionator, on the other hand, has an opinion on every subject in the hollow of his head. The extra message: "Come swim in my oceans of notions. I have opinions about subjects that haven't been raised yet. Look up to and admire my superior idea factory. Therefore, look up to and admire me." The individual with this style often attaches to a mate who is insecure and is attracted to him because she misjudges his superopinionation as evincing a leader who is seeking truth. Sadly, he is less interested in truth than he is in persuading himself that his present notions are the truth.

"DIG ME" STYLE

The "Dig Me" Style is addicted to the double entendre, the double-meaning play on words. He mimics, jokes, finds witticisms in the most obscure places no matter how deeply serious the discussion—translates laughter of others into love for himself. The extra message: "See how I entertain and amuse you. I'm your court jester. I'm selling you barrels of laughs for just a cup of love. Now, don't you at least like me?"

There are countless other quasi-belonging styles in addition to those described above, and it is possible to find a number of various styles in the same individual. I'm sure the reader recognizes the incompleteness and abbreviated nature of these style descriptions. There are many other qualities such as empathy, diligence, thoughtfulness, laziness, honesty, and dishonesty that can be present in any individual with any of the styles outlined.

Quasi-belonging styles are found both in and out of marriage, but I believe that in marriage, contrasting styles attract each other. It appears that a person with a particular style unconsciously feeds his counterpart his special fare in return for vicariously filling the holes in his own personality. For example, I've never seen a sadist living with a sadist. I've seen sadists living with masochists, Super-Self-sufficient Styles with Fawn in the Forest Styles and dominating styles with subservient styles.

For the past ten years I have followed, with considerable interest, the constancy that men with obsessive-compulsive styles marry women with impulsive, hysterical styles. I have resolutely chosen not to report this finding before now, due to one of the habits I jealously guard in my own style—concentrated dillydallying. The person with a compulsive style is characterized by domination of thinking over feelings, whereas the hysterical style is just the opposite. The compulsive style is detail-conscious; the hysterical style is not. The compulsive style is logical and well organized;

the hysterical style, flighty and impulsive. The compulsive style lives in a world of "shoulds" (I am doing what I'm doing because I should do it) and is predictable, planning everything he does before he does it. I sometimes wonder if he doesn't plan his spontaneity. The hysterical style lives in a world of "wants," is unpredictable and spontaneous. The compulsive style manifests a restriction of attention, getting the job *done,* and abhors distractions. The hysterical style adores distractions and contentedly flits from one thing to another and often from one flirtation to another—and thus these two styles compliment and support each other, like a couple of cooked asparagus stalks.

Quasi-belonging is born of fear—fear of the assumed consequences if one were to reveal his separateness, his own unrepeated, unique individuality. The assumption is: "If I expose my singular identity, how I think and how I feel, I might be rejected, disapproved, or unloved. Therefore, I unconsciously adopt some way of hiding my unique self from others and, unfortunately, from myself as well. I now habitually clothe myself in a psychological camouflage such as 'compliant nice guy' or 'playing authentic' or 'seductive sexpot' or whatever, predicated on my particular background of experiences. My unconscious direction is the disowning of my own personality by staging an illusion of belonging with whoever is with me at the moment. My vehicle for effecting this fusion is a complement of extra nonverbal messages which I transmit along with my verbal communication. If I learn to project messages of helplessness, I can fuse with a helper. If I demonstrate subserviency, I can fuse with a dominator. If I exhibit myself as a sufferer, I can fuse with a healer or, in some cases, a punisher. If I communicate as a little girl, I can fuse with a big daddy."

One of these quasi-belonging styles may remind you of someone seeking your approval. Or one of the styles may touch your own way of trying to belong with others. In any case, I invite you not to indulge in the thankless task of berating yourself or others. It's a waste of energy. Picture someone with the Chameleon Style, trying to find out what is expected of him so he can comply and be accepted by you. You can use your energy experiencing boredom or derision with him if you choose, but this in no way modifies the style. Or consider the person with the Toilet Bowl Syndrome. You can use your energy experiencing amusement or impatience with him if you choose. But it doesn't help him and it doesn't help you. He's hurting, perhaps not so much from the various situations that he complains about as from the prison of his way of belonging, trying to make a bridge of complaints between you and him. He wants to belong so much, to span the gulf between the two of you, but he just doesn't know how to go about it. So what does one do to be truly loved and accepted by others? How does one discard those old habits of *trying* to be loved? How does one move in the direction of becoming the beautiful person he was before he learned these quasi-belonging habits?

I have seen many individuals *unlearn* these habits and move from being poorly accepted to being well accepted. It is how they accomplish this that I wish to share with you in the ensuing chapters.

3
Owning Yourself

IF YOU WANT TO LEARN HOW TO ACTUAL-BELONG
—that is, if you want to be loved and accepted by others
and by yourself—you must first learn how to part with
your present habits of quasi-belonging. And you can't
do this without knowing what these habits are in the first
place. This process of recognizing your present habits of
trying to belong, of having the self introduced to the
self, is what I like to call *owning yourself*.

Owning yourself, taking full responsibility for your
thoughts and words, is the core principle of moving
toward actual-belonging. Owning yourself means, "I
blame no one for my feelings, my thoughts, or my
communication of these thoughts and feelings. I own

them all." For example, when I am owning myself, I don't say to myself, "She frustrates me" or "She makes me mad" or "He makes me cry" or "I *lost* my temper," as though my temper is separate from me. Rather, when I honestly own myself I say, "I frustrate myself" or "I am having a temper tantrum. I choose to yell at you. I elect to use sarcastic words and snarl tones. I choose to glare at you—all because I want to scare you or cause you pain. This all belongs to me. It's all mine. I own it."

The following initial session with a new student* clarifies this idea of "owning yourself." Observe how unaccustomed this individual is to take responsibility for her thoughts or words. The extra nonverbal message is in brackets.

DR. B.: *What is the purpose of your visit today?*

STUDENT: *My husband said I should come.* [You can't hold me accountable for being here; my husband is responsible.]

DR. B.: *You mean that if it were up to you that you wouldn't be here right now?*

STUDENT: *Oh, no, I'd have come.*

DR. B.: *For what reason?*

STUDENT: *My husband says . . . I don't know how to begin.* [I don't want to take responsibility for my words. Ask me something.]

---

* I see these interactions not as a doctor-patient relationship, since the mind is not being treated, but rather as a teacher-student relationship, since learning is going on.

DR. B.: *This is a new experience for you, isn't it?*

STUDENT: *Yes.*

DR. B.: *Do you feel a little tense right now?*

STUDENT: *Oh, no. You don't make me tense.* [I don't want to own my tension. I don't want to risk your disapproval of me.]

DR. B.: *I don't believe I do either. Even so, it would seem that you'd be entitled to some tension in a new experience like this—nothing wrong in that.*

STUDENT: *Well, I do feel tense. I don't know where to begin. I don't know what I should do in here.* [See how helpless I am. Tell me what I should do.]

DR. B.: *This may sound strange, but there's nothing that you* should *do in here. Is there something going on in your life that's unhappy for you?*

STUDENT: *People make me nervous. I don't know why it is, but they just do.* [It's not me. It's the people that do it.]

DR. B.: *Like right now?*

STUDENT: *Yes. I don't know what you want.* [You're to blame for my being nervous. If you'd just take the responsibility of telling me what to do, then I wouldn't be nervous.]

DR. B.: *If you knew what people wanted you to do, then you wouldn't feel nervous?*

STUDENT: *I guess so.* [You can't hold me to this. I just said "I guess so," like maybe, perhaps. I'm not totally responsible, fully owning what I just said.]

DR. B.: *How long have you been experiencing nervousness like this?*

STUDENT: *My husband says it's been like this just lately.* [I don't own this communication. It's my husband who said it, not me.]

DR. B.: *Would you agree with him?*

STUDENT: *Yes.* [Taking responsibility, owning her communication.]

Following is how the preceding dialogue would take place were the student to own herself:

DR. B.: *What is the purpose of your visit today?*

STUDENT: *I've been feeling tense lately when I'm around people.*

The above sentence provides the same information as the eleven sentences of the student's previous dialogue.

Ultimately, the whole question of learning to actual-belong through the medium of owning yourself revolves about Einstein's principle of the finite nature of relative energy. You're not a bottomless well of energies and therefore, if, out of habit, you pour gallon after gallon of your life energy into a situation in anger, worry, frustration, or self-consciousness, which really is entitled to no more than half a pint, then you are depleting those energies that you might use for more constructive purposes. Didn't you ever wonder how it is that some people seem to achieve so much more than others in their lifetime, how some seem so much more peaceful than others?

There's nothing mysterious about it. Some simply have learned to use their allotment of energies more constructively than others. And this is what I'm inviting you to do through the principle of owning yourself.

Imagine yourself coming late to a small meeting, with everyone, all strangers, looking at you as you walk across the room to a chair. What kind of feelings do you produce in yourself? Notice I don't ask, "What kind of feelings do the strangers produce in you?" Because they don't produce feelings in you. They are a *condition* that you may use for whatever feelings you may be in the habit of producing in yourself. Do you feel self-conscious as you walk across the room? Will you own your self-consciousness or will you tend to blame your self-conscious feeling on the people there? If the people were really responsible for your self-conscious feeling, then they would be able to make *every*one self-conscious under the same circumstances. The fact is that many individuals will not produce these self-conscious feelings in themselves. Some will use their energies angering themselves because the meeting started without them. Some will worry themselves lest they missed something. Some would not come in at all by making themselves afraid that the leader might disapprove of their lateness. Some will frustrate themselves with the idea that they are interrupting the meeting, and still others will do none of these but will be glad that they finally arrived. Thus one doesn't have to behave as an automaton. When he owns himself, he can see there is an array of options open to him, other than his accustomed way of behaving.

The following audio-taped group session deals with owning yourself and actual-belonging. The extra, nonverbal messages will be in brackets.

Carl is the focus of the session at this point. Two of the members are remarking about his voice, which has a lilting, gentle, noneffeminate, and exceedingly accepting tone.

CARL: *I felt some little bit of hostility when you commented on my taking notes. Can you remember that? I felt very defensive because I felt bad that I was taking notes. Do you remember that?*

DON: *No, I remember earlier when the session started my reaction to you was . . . nebulous. Do you want me to give that reaction?*

CARL: *Sure, I'd like you to.*

DON: *The way you talk seems like you're trying to be super nice.*

CARL: *Right now, you mean?*

DON: *Generally.*

CARL: *Okay.*

DON: *. . . And I'm curious as to how you are ordinarily —if you are different than how you are in here. Is this the way you always are?*

CARL: *I think I try to be nicer elsewhere.*

DON: (Not waiting for Carl to finish—irritation in his voice.) *It's your tone that bothers me, and maybe that's where you detected hostility. I felt some hostility toward*

Brian also because he seems to be away from us. Maybe
it's because I want to know you both and I don't know
you in some way because of your facade. ["I don't
choose to own my anger. It's your *facade* that is to
blame. I choose to use this snarl term, 'facade,' because
I want to cause you pain. But how can you possibly
reject me since I've said I *want* to know you?" (Disowning
of self.)]

DORA: *I—I sense the same thing. That—that—same—*
that—tone of voice, I—I felt the same way you did.
I just, it just—oh, God, are you for real? (Looks up at
ceiling with an expression of derision) [Her tone of
voice is belittling and scornful. Her extra message is:
"We can belong with each other, you and me, Don, as
we gang up on Carl together. Oh, how I love kicking
him while he's down."]

DR. B.: *Dora, your choice of words, your tone, and the*
expression on your face are like porcupine quills. Will
you own your communication right now? Are you
trying to hurt Carl?

DORA: *No, I'm not.* ["If I owned choosing such snarl
words and scornful tone, then I wouldn't be accepted."
(Quasi-belonging with the group)]

DR. B.: *Then that's significant, Dora—something to*
own—perhaps a habit of unconsciously selecting words,
tones, and facial expressions that can hurt but without
a conscious awareness of intent to hurt. Will you own
this?

DORA: (Not listening) *No, it's not, I was—I—I'm not trying to hurt you.* ["Don't disapprove of me." Dora is pouring so much energy into her struggle to be accepted that she doesn't have any left to listen, to own herself, and to acknowledge herself in a friendly way. There's no further pushing of this process with Dora at this time because everyone grows at his own pace in his own good time.]

DON: (Turning to Dr. B.) *May I ask Carl a question?* [Meek tone: "How can you not accept me as polite and submissive as I am?"]

DR. B.: (Smiling) *You didn't say "Sir."* [Don has been invited to own his submissive approach to me in a previous session.]

DON: (Chuckling and moving his hand as to push me away.) *I don't need your permission.* [Here he is *owning in a friendly way* his temporary submissiveness.] *Carl, did I hurt you when I said what I said?* [No manipulation for acceptance here; this is a request for information.]

CARL: *I felt hurt because I felt I was wrong taking the notes. Uh, I didn't realize you meant to hurt me, though. I didn't feel you did at the time.* ["Let's have nothing come between us. It's my fault for taking notes. It's me who is wrong." Here Carl disowns his separateness, his freedom to take notes.]

DON: (Turning to Dr. B.) *Is there—did you feel I was trying to hurt him?* [Here Don is owning his communication no matter what the answer.]

DR. B.: *Yes, both you and Dora, but I don't know if it were conscious intent though. You're invited and*

*encouraged to express your thoughts and feelings—
but I'm suggesting that you not stop there, that you own
the words you choose to communicate. It's only then
that you're in a position of deciding whether you want
to retain these habits or discard them.*

TOM: *But suppose I really want to hurt someone?* [Tom
is owning himself here with a genuine question.]

DR. B.: *Yes, exactly—own that. The point is you're not
a machine. A machine can't own itself—take full
responsibility for what it's doing and then decide to
reprogram itself to make better use of its energies. You
can. You have that power. You can own using words
like—what was your word, Don?—facade?*

DON: *Yeah.*

DR. B.: *Or, "God, are you for real?"—you can own these
and say to yourself, "These are my thoughts, my
feelings, my words. No one forces me to be this way or
that." Now you're in a position to either pretend you're
a machine with no power over your destiny or to own
your free humanness and do almost anything you want
with yourself.*

TOM: *Are you suggesting I should never hurt anyone?*
[Here Tom is not owning himself, by presenting his
opinion disguised as a question.]

DR. B.: *I'm sure if someone is attacking your family, you
aren't going to assume the lotus position and meditate.
There are appropriate times for the way you choose to
use your energies. What I'm paying attention to here is
that you can own yourself no matter what your choice.
For example, Carl's vocal tones don't make Don angry.*

*It is Don who makes Don angry. Here he's invited to own
that feeling and see if he wants to continue using his
energies in this direction.*

DON: *I asked you if you thought I was hurting Carl
because in my relationships outside I do have a way of
hurting. I know, because sometimes I get really bad
reactions from people when I didn't know I was hurting
them. I was trying to be matter-of-fact and I've realized
I've said something that really crushed them.* [Congruent
owning of self]

DORA: *Yes, I've done that.* (Softly) *I guess I still do.*
[Congruent owning of self]

TOM: *My wife and I hurt each other sometimes and I
don't know why we do that.* [Owning of self]

DR. B.: *I believe that when we try to hurt someone,
we're hurting ourselves—our insides, whether we call it
our mind or soul or whatever, whether it's unconscious
on our part or not. And I think that when our aim is to
hurt someone, we begin to form a habit, since it becomes
easier to do it the next time. It gradually becomes a
part of our character as we immunize ourselves against
others' pain. For example, I'm convinced that married
couples cooperate in their discord. It takes just as much
cooperation to be discordant as it does to be harmonious.
The trouble is that they don't realize how they cooperate
with one another in producing discord, since their actions
are so habitual and unconscious. They haven't been
exposed to the concept of owning themselves and
realizing they have a choice.*

CARL: *I like that—that we have a choice to hurt or not
hurt, to even feel hurt or not.* [Owning of self—
actual-belonging]

46

The following dialogue is between a husband and wife:

JILL: (Tears, pouting) *You're always putting me down, trying to make me look like a fool.*

JACK: *I'm too late. Mother Nature beat me to it.*

JILL: (More tears)

JACK: (Angry tone) *You frustrate the hell out of me. How many times do I have to tell you—I want a big apple in my lunch, not a small one.*

In this dialogue neither participant owns his thoughts, words, or feelings. Each is choosing to manipulate the other and in the process of that choice, opts to sacrifice his own self-respect and dignity. If Jack and Jill were to own themselves, they would acknowledge respectively that Jack cannot put Jill down without her 100 percent cooperation and Jill cannot frustrate Jack without his cooperation. Further, Jill would take full responsibility for her tears, her pouting, and her seeking to coerce Jack into feeling guilty. And Jack, in turn, would take full responsibility for his yelling, his frustrating himself, and his desire to cause Jill pain.

The reason I refer to *owning yourself* as the core principle in actual-belonging is that it is essential that you own yourself, that is, get acquainted with your *present* habits of behavior before you can make choices as to which habits to discard or retain. The technique for learning to own yourself is what I refer to as *checking-in.*

4
Checking-in, Checking-out

FANTASIZE THAT YOU OWN A REMARKABLE VEHICLE in which you are traveling away from earth at a rate considerably faster than the speed of light, about 186,000 miles per second. Attached to your vehicle is an extremely powerful audio-telescope. After a short period of travel at this speed, stop and direct your powerful audio-telescope to observe and listen to yourself on earth. You can do this because your image, from one point to another, can only travel at the speed of light while your vehicle, with you in it, has been traveling at a rate faster than the speed of light. You can travel well out into space, stop at various points, turn your audio-telescope back toward earth, and see prehistoric people, or the Crusades, or Columbus landing. Or you could see yourself at any given moment from birth to now. For the moment, fantasize turning the audio-telescope on yourself at a time when you are frustrating yourself and having a temper tantrum. Select such a moment now. Don't try to remember it but, rather, close your eyes and see it in your mind's eye. Stay with this moment before reading on.

Now move your vehicle and observe a time when you are enjoying yourself, and stay with this moment in the same way. You wouldn't be able to yell or berate or congratulate yourself on earth. At least it wouldn't have much effect, since you couldn't hear yourself at that distance anyway. All you can do is look and listen to yourself—nothing more. You couldn't even ask yourself, "Why on earth are you doing what you're doing?" But you can observe *what* you're doing and *how* you're doing it.

In essence, this is what checking-in is—a dispassionate vehicle for owning yourself, a friendly acknowledging, without condemnation or commendation, as though you are objectively perceiving yourself from your space vehicle.

There are four elements to checking-in. You can experience them right now:

Physical Sensations

Check-in to your physical self. What are you doing to the muscles of your abdomen, neck, or face? Are you relaxing or tensing them?

Emotional Feelings

Check-in to your psychological feelings. What kind of feelings are you producing in yourself right now? How do you do that? Are you generating feelings that are calm? anxious? guilty? pressured? free? angry? You'll notice you can produce more than one feeling at any given moment.

Attitude

Check-in to how you think. Think about some person right now. Are you choosing to think negatively? positively? judgmentally? Or in an accepting way?

Communications System

Check-in to how you communicate these thoughts and feelings. What does your tone of voice say to others? What kind of words do you choose? What do you communicate with your eyes? Your hands?

The magic words of checking-in are *how* and *what*. *How* am I belonging with this person right now? *What* is the extra message I may be sending? Am I pitifully pouting, burrowing into his heart, and gouging a chunk of compassion for his acceptance of me? Am I coercing him with my stabbing sarcasms to think as I think? Am I belly-laughing at a mediocre joke to extract the approval of the joke teller? Am I being super agreeable to keep him glued to me? Am I brandishing my intellectuality to attract his admiration of me? Am I straining to find out what he expects of me so that I can comply, thus buying his acceptance of me? Am I displaying how helpless and indecisive I am, milking his help? Or am I actual-belonging by not manipulating anyone in any way for his or her acceptance, approval, or love for me?

The following dialogue between a student and myself will clarify the principle of checking-in. Note that the student is able to own whether he is actual-belonging or quasi-belonging at any given moment.

DR. B.: *Just now, while I've been talking, you've been looking at me most intently. Will you check-in and tell me what you're aware of, the intensity of your gaze?*

STUDENT: *I'm aware of listening to you—listening hard.*

DR. B.: *Is there anything else you're aware of as you check-in?*

STUDENT: *Just that I don't want to miss anything.*

DR. B.: *Can you sense in any way your trying to curry my favor as a good, attentive student?*

STUDENT: *No, not in the least.*

DR. B.: *I don't sense it either; that is, I don't sense that you are trying to manipulate me to gain my approval. And that's actual-belonging.*

STUDENT: *It would be foolish for anyone to appear as a good student just so you'd approve of them.*

DR. B.: *Check-in now. What extra message may you be sending now?*

STUDENT: (After a few seconds pause) *I want you to know* (laughter)—*I want you to know that I'm not foolish like others—that I'm a good student.* (Much laughter from both the student and Dr. B.)

DR. B.: (Still laughing) *You're trying to coax some approval out of me—trying to impress on me that you're a good student—even though you know it's easier to look good when you don't try so hard to look good.*

STUDENT: *Yes, I'm trying to get you to—*(much laughing).

DR. B.: *And that's quasi-belonging. Every time you catch yourself manipulating me or someone else for approval or love, that's quasi-belonging. But you wouldn't know or be able to own that if you hadn't checked in. Now check-in again to your last communication where you were laughing and saying something like "Yes, I'm trying to get you to—."*

STUDENT: (Excited) *That's spontaneous. I'm not trying to get your approval there—or trying to look good. It's just funny catching myself. It's fun.*

DR. B.: *That's what I experience, too. It's fun enjoying something together—actual-belonging. Now will you check-in again? How does that feel inside when you discover you're not trying to get me to approve of you— when you're spontaneously actual-belonging?*

STUDENT: *One thing, it's a good feeling. I feel better about myself—like cleaner. That's it, I feel cleaner about myself and lighter.*

DR. B.: *Great feeling, isn't it, discovering your genuineness. Now as you check-in to the entire interaction between us, how do you experience the whole process? What is it?*

STUDENT: *You mean, how do I feel about it?*

DR. B.: *No. What are we doing here, you and I? How are you relating to me and how am I relating to you?*

STUDENT: *Well, I'm learning, and—it's a student-teacher thing.*

DR. B: *Would you call that actual-belonging or quasi-belonging?*

STUDENT: *I believe it's actual.*

DR. B.: *Now fantasize me belonging like this outside of session. Suppose I were teaching all the time, always forcing my information on others. Then what?*

STUDENT: *I think that would be quasi-belonging.*

DR. B.: *I do, too. In here it's appropriate, but outside of here it would be inordinate—consistently trying to manipulate others for their acceptance. The extra message—and there's always an extra message in quasi-belonging—would be, "See how I'm the eternal guru, how easily I see through people. Now, don't you admire my mind and accept me?"*

I believe that self-respect is the reinforcer for actual-belonging. Each time the student checks-in and discovers he is actual-belonging, the good feeling, or as the student said, the "clean feeling," of self-respect acts as a rewarding conditioner that influences him to actual-belong again and again.

Checking-in is making conscious what was unconscious. Some of the questions you can ask yourself when checking-in are as follows:

How do I feel with this person right now? Do I make myself comfortable or uncomfortable? If uncomfortable, in what way do I do that? Do I tighten my abdominal muscles, my neck muscles? Do I make myself queasy or quivery inside? Do I dart my eyes or do I often look down? Am I so frightening myself that I make my heart pound? Do I make my palms sweaty, my mouth dry? Do I constantly keep my hands moving or do I make a fist? Will I own all these muscles as mine, these feelings, these thoughts, these words? Or do I refuse to acknowledge my responsibility for my thoughts and subsequent actions?

How do I feel toward this person? Critical? Competitive? Sympathetic? Impatient? Accepting? Fearful? Loving? How do I look at him? As an adversary? As interesting? As a diversion? As boring? As delightful? As a challenge? As a potential admirer?

Do I separate people according to whether they are believers or nonbelievers? Do I feel condescending and smug because he hasn't found the truth I have? Do I

*feel critical because he smokes or drinks or uses language
I'm not accustomed to? Or do I neither condemn nor
condone, but see him as just another creature like me
who wants to belong as much as I do?*

*How do I look at this person right now? What are my
vocal intonations? What kind of words do I choose? Do
my feelings, thoughts, and words all go down the same
track or do I send two messages at the same time, one
verbal and the other nonverbal?*

*Am I trying to manipulate this person into accepting or
loving me by showing him how smart I am? How modest
I am? How sexy I am? How funny I am? How agreeable
I am? How manly I am? How authentic I am? Do I
speak only when spoken to? Do I dominate conversations?
Am I genuinely interested in this person or can I hardly
wait until he's finished talking so that I can make my
point? What do I often talk about? Is gossip my daily
fare? Is sex my main topic, or is it about what a hard life
I'm having? Is my subject matter usually philosophical,
generalizing about this and that? Am I often defensive
or offensive? Are my words, thoughts, feelings and
intonations all going down the same track at the same
time? Am I direct or indirect in how I communicate?
Does the other person know where I really stand? Am I
telling him how I really feel? Do I seldom forget myself
and attend to how he is feeling and how he is thinking?*

Of all these questions, the one that I believe is crucial
to actual-belonging is: "Am I communicating directly
right now?" And this implicitly includes the idea: "Am
I listening carefully right now?"

Oblique communication, or communicating at an angle, I believe, is the most successful method yet developed by couples for not resolving anything. Following is an example of this form of communication:

JOAN: *Tom, do you think this dress is too formal for the PTA?*

TOM: *Well, it's a nice dress, and you look good in blue.*

JOAN: *I mean, do you think it's too formal for that meeting?*

TOM: *Well, I like it better than the other blue one. When is the meeting?*

JOAN: *It's tonight, Tom. We decided to go last week. Remember?*

TOM: *Oh, damn. I'll miss the play-offs on TV.*

JOAN: *Tom, how about the dress? Do you think it's too formal or not?*

TOM: *I already told you. I like it.*

JOAN: *I like it, too, but I just want to know if you think I should wear it to the PTA meeting, if it's too formal or not.*

TOM: *Why not? You like it, too, don't you?*

JOAN: *Yes* (a little exasperated), *but it might be too formal for that kind of meeting.*

TOM: *You think so?*

JOAN: *Oh, Tom—I'm not sure. That's why I asked your opinion.*

TOM: *Well, I always did like it whether it's too formal or not.*

JOAN: (Resigned) *Let's get ready, Tom. We'll be late.*

TOM: *You going to wear that dress?*

JOAN: *No, Tom. I decided to wear your jockey shorts.*

TOM: *What are you talking about?*

Joan, in the above dialogue, is requesting that Tom actual-belong with her as a mature decision-making couple. But to do so, Tom would be revealing his unique, separate self which, incidentally, doesn't happen to know whether the dress is too formal or not but it's hard for him to say, "I don't know." Tom unconsciously chooses to quasi-belong to Joan by communicating obliquely with her, as though she is asking him if he *likes* the dress or not, thus not risking her looking down on him as naïve or uninformed. If Tom checked-in and owned his communication, he would be in a position to discard his indirect communication. His *direct* communication to Joan would be, "Is it too formal? I don't know the answer to that, Joan, but you look so well in it, why not take a chance and wear it anyway."

Regular checking-in gradually eliminates quasi-belonging habits. The process of parting with unwanted behavior is threefold, whether it's a way of thinking, feeling, or communicating. At first it's "There, I did it again." A few days or weeks later it's "There, I almost did it again." And in a few more weeks it's "I can remember when I used to do that."

When you do modify your way of thinking, interestingly enough, your way of feeling and communicating are likewise affected. Modify your way of feeling, and your way of thinking and communicating are affected; modify your way of communicating, and your way of thinking and feeling tag along.

Checking-in is not done twenty minutes after the fact. It's done at the very moment of the event. (Am I being defensive right now? Am I being indirect now? Am I interested in how this person feels right now? Am I trying to manipulate this person's approval of me right now?) The usual time required for checking-in is from one to five seconds. If you do it one hundred times a day, therefore, you're using six or seven minutes of your day. Sadly enough, many people go through their lifetime with hardly any checking-in. Consequently, they barely know themselves.

When Franklin checks-in, he becomes more aware of his compassion for others. When he checks-in further, he discovers that he rarely *expresses* this compassion *to* others. In a taped group session Franklin made some further discoveries.

DR. B.: *Franklin, will you finish this idea: "If I let you all see how compassionate I am, then . . ." Check-in and then finish it.*

FRANKLIN: *. . . then you'll all see what a softie I am.*

DR. B.: *Will you check-in some more as to how you think. "If you all could see how soft I am, then . . ."*

FRANKLIN: *If you all could see what a softie I am, then, then, uh, well—then you could put me down. Women are softies and I'm not a woman.*

NOTE: Here Franklin's quasi-belonging style includes hiding his own separate feelings, manipulating others to see him *not* as he really is but as he believes he must be seen by others in order to be accepted. He tells himself that for him to be accepted by others he must come across as a real man. He further tells himself that a real man doesn't reveal feelings of compassion.

JANE: *Gentle men appeal to me, Franklin.*

GROUP: (Much agreement with Jane from both men and women)

DR. B.: *Franklin, would you like to do something about your inhibiting yourself like this? The extra message seems to be: "Notice how I'm not a softie, I'm a man. Now you can't put me down. You can't reject me." It well may be that this habit of stifling expression of these feelings is also stifling others being attracted to you. Do you want to do something about it?*

FRANKLIN: *Yeah, let's go. That's what I'm here for.*

DR. B.: *Okay. A moment ago when Dan was telling Carol how she rarely looks at anyone when she's talking, you were looking hard at Dan. Can you reflect on that look and recall your feelings?*

FRANKLIN: *Yes.* (Silence; looking down at rug)

DR. B.: *For the next few seconds, would you communicate as if you're not fearful of being put down. This is a little experiment and we'll see where it goes from there.*

FRANKLIN: (Clearing throat—silence) *Well, Dan, this is only the second time Carol's been in the group and— and—well, I think it's too early and too much to be confronting her right now.* (Big sigh)

GROUP: (Applauding—much affirmation)

DAN: *I really didn't attack her. Did you think I attacked you, Carol?*

JILL: (Not waiting for Carol to respond) *Franklin didn't say you attacked Carol, just that he felt it was too soon to confront a new member. What I'd like to say is that I feel you just gave me some of yourself, Franklin— and if you call it "softie," well, I like it. There's . . .*

GEORGE: *I don't think it's being a "softie," whatever that is. I was thinking, I don't—I think it took some courage to say what you did.*

FRANKLIN: *Boy, did it ever. I don't say things like that. And I'm not accusing you of attacking Carol, Dan. See, that's the thing—like this—that can happen when I say something like that.* [Franklin is referring to his asserting some feeling of compassion.]

DR. B.: *Carol, will you check-in right now? What's going on? What are you doing with yourself?*

CAROL: *You mean what I'm thinking right now?*

DR. B.: *Yes, that and how you're feeling about others and how you're feeling about yourself—even what your stomach is doing, or more accurately, what you may be doing to your stomach.*

CAROL: *Well, I know I've got butterflies in my stomach and I'm scared being in here—but not nearly as much as before Franklin said what he did.*

DR. B.: *Will you check-in, Carol. What's going on inside of you with respect to Franklin?*

CAROL: *Well, I admire his . . .*

DR. B.: *Tell him, Carol. It's a little harder to communicate directly with someone rather than talking about him.*

CAROL: *Franklin, I admire you for what you did and I appreciate it. I mean, I appreciate you. I don't want to look like I need protecting, but I really appreciate you.*

GROUP: (Much affirmation)

DR. B.: *Will you check-in right now, Franklin. Where are you?*

FRANKLIN: *I feel—I don't know if I'm—I feel a little proud of myself.*

DR. B.: *It was like you really had to gather yourself to do this unaccustomed thing.*

FRANKLIN: *Yeah.*

DR. B.: *Check-in once more. Do you feel any less of a man?*

FRANKLIN: *No—no, dammit—more. Well, I don't know. It's not that I feel more or less of a man. There's something good inside—feeling proud.*

DR. B.: *This "good" feeling—check-in with the idea of self-respect. Does that fit at all?*

FRANKLIN: *Yeah, in a way. Yeah, it does—and like excited.*

DR. B.: *You used the words "softie" and "man." Maybe what you're saying now is that there's no manliness or womanliness involved. Perhaps the good feeling comes from just being human and having the courage to let others see this and love you all the more because of it. This is only a practice field in here. Go out and have some fun expressing compassionate feelings whenever you want—even to your wife and kids.*

GROUP: (Much laughing)

In the above engagement, Franklin took the first step toward modifying his thinking about what constitutes a *man.* Subsequently, his feelings about this and his way of communicating compassion were affected. Through repetition, this way of thinking, feeling, and communicating will become a part of him. It all began with checking-in and owning his behavior and then taking that first step to part with his former habit of inhibiting himself.

There are a number of things that can encourage a person's journey to actual-belonging—to being loved. The cohesiveness of the group is one of them. I'm convinced that the concept of some "encounter" groups that encourage people to vent their hostile feelings toward each other in the name of therapy is open to serious reexamination. In my judgment the more cohesive a group, that is, the more each actual-belongs, deriving satisfaction from the satisfaction of others and experiencing a joy in the growth of others, the more quickly will each member of the group develop. A second growth factor, one that defies measurement, is the *unconscious* process of moving toward actual-belonging. As I watch the members of a group saying their good-byes at the end of a session and see the fleeting signs of unadulterated love on some of their faces, I know that they will never again be quite the same. Some nebulous something has rubbed off on each of us. The activities of this kind of group could be referred to as *belonging training* or, in more traditional terms, *belonging therapy*.

The third and final thing that contributes to learning how to actual-belong is a *conscious* process, available to any reader who chooses to use it. Four steps are involved: *desire, expectancy, behaving as if,* and *reinforcement*. Without a desire to grow, to experience the excitement of actual-belonging, there is little progress. Check-in to yourself right now, if you will. How much desire do you have? The first step is a must.

The second step is *expectancy*. If you have a desire to learn to play a violin, you don't just hope you'll learn how to play. You *expect* that, with practice, you *will* learn. Likewise, you don't merely *hope* that you will learn to be less self-conscious, or more assertive, or less defensive, or more direct, or whatever. You *expect* that with practice—learning to check-in and own yourself completely and not blaming others for how you think— you *will* learn to be more assertive and direct.

The third step is *behaving as if.* The very first time you hold the violin in the proper position with the bow resting across the strings, no one can tell whether you've been playing it for twenty weeks or twenty minutes. For instance, the very next time Franklin expresses a compassionate feeling, no one can tell whether he's been doing it all his life or if it's the very first time.

The final step is *reinforcement.* As you practice the violin, the arpeggios, the up-bow and down-bow staccato, the vibrato, you arrive at a point where you no longer know how *not* to play it. As you practice being more direct, or expressing compassionate feelings, you arrive at a point where you no longer know how not to be that way. It's part of your substance and is constantly being *reinforced* through sheer repetition. The four steps, mnemonically, spell out the word *dear. D* for desire, *E* for expectancy, *A* for behaving as if, and *R* for reinforcement.

There's no special time to check-in. You can practice it at any moment of the day, whether you're with someone or alone. You can practice it when you're sunning yourself or worrying yourself, relaxing yourself or tensing yourself, or whatever. The point is to stop, look, and listen to yourself and *own* yourself at that instant in your inner space. You can do it right this second with this book you're reading. Right now ask yourself, "How do I feel about this book? Do I feel bored? Do I feel tense? Confused? Excited? Irritated? How am I thinking? Is my mind elsewhere? Am I agreeing with the author or disagreeing? How do these attitudes influence what I am reading? Am I seeking truth or am I persuading myself that my present notions are the truth? Am I pressuring myself to read as quickly as possible so that I can get on to other things? Do I really want to continue using my energies this way?

A curious phenomenon occurs when you check-in and discover a negative experience, such as unexplained tension. As you get in tune with the tension and heighten your awareness of your sweaty palms, your butterfly stomach, your tightened neck muscles, there is almost invariably a diminishing of the whole tension process. I don't know why this is. Possibly it has something to do with the simple acknowledgment that one is tensing himself and then not fighting it but facing it without fear. Perhaps it's analogous to putting something out on the wash line in the sun and letting evaporation take its natural course. In any event, there seem to be considerably more energies expended in fearing a negative experience than in facing it with an attitude of objectivity.

Conversely, when you check-in to a positive experience, such as sexual intercourse, there is usually an enhancement of pleasure. Checking-in to this experience is checking-in to the tactile sense. It's a losing of the mind and coming to the senses, attuning yourself to the skin-to-skin contact, especially attending to what and how you are feeling in the area of the genitalia. There is no worrying such as "Oh, I hope it doesn't go down" or "Oh, I wonder if I'll have an orgasm this time" or "Gosh, I wonder if I'm pleasing her [or him]; I hope

I am but maybe I'm not." I'm convinced that the ideal way to consistently have unsuccessful intercourse is to always introspect (think, think, think) and never check-in.

I've often heard a beginning student ask, "If I check-in so much, won't I become self-conscious?" Self-consciousness is almost the opposite of checking-in. Self-consciousness, the mildest form of paranoia, is a self-induced mini-delusion that is dependent on the grandiose idea that "everyone who is looking at me is thinking about me." Checking-in, conversely, is not thinking in terms of interpretation, analyzing or rationalizing. It is pure observation. Self-consciousness is born of fear and assumptions and needs another person in order to exist. Checking-in is a product of curiosity and can be done at will with or without another person.

Sometimes politicians and big-business men give themselves all kinds of reasons for choosing not to look too closely at the consequences of their behavior on others. One such individual said to me, "If I looked too closely at that, I might not like what I see," so he didn't. I believe that those who choose not to look too closely at the effects of their behavior, such as self-consciousness, on themselves and others are no less deceiving of themselves. However, neither consciously knows of this deception because the process is kept out of awareness. Most individuals who practice self-consciousness religiously have little awareness of the extent of the consequences of their behavior on others. They don't know how uncomfortable others feel around them because no one tells them. I sometimes wonder if a self-conscious person has an aura that permeates the atmosphere, since, no matter how he may try to hide it, others sense his tightness and embarrassment, and secretly wish he would stop it, or leave.

Self-consciousness is a learned process. Babies are not born self-conscious. In fact, some of them don't even care if they have clothes on or not. However, parents are models for their children's behavior and the children unwittingly learn how to be self-conscious by observing a parent. Happily, however, whatever is learned can be unlearned. I've seen many individuals step out of their tight, self-conscious world and become as little children again without those constricting psychological garments.

Checking-in is a sensing process. You use your eyes. What am I doing with my body? Am I in perpetual motion when I talk or am I almost immobile? What bodily posture do I choose? What gait? What clothes? You use your ears. What intonations do I choose? Are they condescending? Childlike? Burdensome? Sonorous? Seductive? What words do I choose? Are they sarcastic or friendly? Do I habitually complain or rarely complain? Am I often defending myself or offending others? Am I being direct or indirect? Am I choosing to be impatient, patient, irritable, or peaceful right now?

Whenever you check-in and catch yourself doing any of the above, bear in mind that simultaneously you are communicating that very thing to whoever is with you at the moment. The message you send by how you walk, dress, feel, or think is communicated whether you intend it to be or not. In this sense you're like a ripple on a pond, touching everything in your sphere of contact, reaching shore, and then returning to affect yourself.

Oftentimes, in group session, I've seen an individual check-in, discover he's repeating some unwanted behavior, and then become angry with himself. This contaminates the process, and energies go down the drain which could otherwise have been used for more constructive purposes. It's preferable to acknowledge in a *friendly* way whatever you are discovering in yourself.

Checking-in is a conscious process at first just like learning to type, and gradually, as you practice, the conscious process becomes unconscious and automatic. As you do anything again and again it becomes a part of your person. Each time you check-in and resolve to discard this habit or retain that one, you are getting to know yourself that much better. The more you own yourself—that is, the more you authentically actual-belong with yourself—the better you can actual-belong with others. Your habits of manipulating others to quasi-belong, of struggling for their approval or quaking in the fear of not getting it, tend to melt away and you are more loving and loved.

Actual-belonging is also a function of *checking-out.* Checking-out means that you are heightening your awareness of the other person. As with checking-in, the magic words are *what* and *how*. Checking-out is totally outside the self. It means, "How does this person feel? How does he think? How does he look at me? Does he avert his eyes while he's talking? Could it be that he is feeling uneasy? Does he look at me with a gentle, rested gaze? Could it be that he is feeling calm? Does he look at me out of the corner of his eye? Does this mean he is suspicious? How does he sound? Does he talk with little modulation? Does this indicate excessive control and self-consciousness or is he depressed? Do his vocal tones have considerable range? Is he feeling light and alive? Do his vocal tones trail off at the end of each sentence? Does he feel burdened? How does he listen? Does he manifest interest, picking up everything I say? Does he appear impatient, waiting for me to finish so he can say what he has to say? Does he respond to my questions directly? Does he skirt my question by not quite answering it? How does he think? Does he look at the world through dark-colored glasses, rose-colored glasses, or clear glasses? What are his interests? His joys? His sorrows? Is he kind? Is he gentle?

The crucial aspect of checking-out is that it is *not* judgmental; it is pure observation. You are practicing observing, acknowledging where that person is at this moment with you. And as you practice checking-out, you'll discover you are becoming more expert in perceiving the feelings* and even some of the thoughts of others. You're opening your eyes and ears to the world around you. Now you're not just *talking about* it: "We should be more interested in others." You're *doing* it.

* A UCLA study [1] has shown that comprehension of any feeling transmitted in the course of a conversation is dependent 38 percent on intonations, 55 percent on facial and body expression, and 7 percent on words.

You're observing the interesting and varied way people belong with you, and you're becoming more of a significant person in the life of everyone you touch, especially when you check-out verbally.

The process for checking-out verbally I like to call *withness listening*.* I have divided listening into three types: passive, supportive, and withness. Passive listening is what the medical students or psychiatric residents do when I'm lecturing; they sit passively and look at me. I don't know if they're listening or not. They could be thinking about their golf game, for all I know. Supportive listening is what a psychiatrist may do while you're talking. He can get his head on a rocker and it bobs while you're talking. You still don't know if he's with you, really listening. He looks like he is, as he supportively nods his head in your direction. He could be thinking about his tennis game. *Withness listening* is that kind of listening that lets the other person know with absolute certainty that he is understood. You are listening not only to his words but particularly to his *feelings*, and he knows it because you verbally check-out his feelings at that very moment with him.

The example that follows is between a parent and a nine-year-old boy. He's just returned from school and appears irritated. The first dialogue represents the *usual* mother-son interaction:

* Carl Rogers and Thomas Gordon call this "receptive listening" and "active listening" respectively. I prefer the term "withness listening" because when it is practiced the individuals feel more *with* each other, less judged, and more accepted.

JOHNNY: (Comes into the house with a sad, grumpy expression)

MOM: *What's the matter?*
JOHNNY: *Oh, nothing.*

MOM: *Well, it seems like something is the matter. What is it?*

JOHNNY: *Frank and the others wouldn't let me play kickball with them.*

MOM: *Why not?*

JOHNNY: *They just wouldn't let me play.*

MOM: *Well, did you ask them?*

JOHNNY: *Yeah.*

MOM: *What did they say?*

JOHNNY: *Oh, I don't want to talk about it.*

MOM: *Did you do something so they didn't want you to play?*

JOHNNY: *No.*

MOM: *Well, you must have done something. Something must have happened.*

JOHNNY: (Irritable) *I said I didn't do anything. Anyway, I don't want to talk about it.*

MOM: *If you didn't do anything, then they should have let you play. You got to stick up for yourself in this world, Johnny.*

JOHNNY: *Uh-huh.*

MOM: *It won't do any good to mope around about it. Just forget it and go get washed up.*

JOHNNY: (Looks at Mom for a moment, then turns and leaves)

In this communication system the mother is doing the best she can with the tools she has to work with. There is no checking-out in this exchange. Mother is the interrogator, the adviser, the problem-solver, and the sergeant, in that order.

Following is the same situation where Mom has learned to check-out, using the technique of *withness listening*. Remember that in this method the listener is checking-out not only words but especially feelings, feelings that are usually nonverbal. (Feeling words are in bold-face type.)

MOM: *You sure look* **unhappy**, *Johnny. You seem* **irritated** *by something.*

JOHNNY: *Yeah, I thought we were all going to play kickball after school and I didn't get to play.*

MOM: *That must have been* **disappointing**.

JOHNNY: *Yeah. Frank and the others wouldn't let me play with them.*

MOM: *And you felt* **left out**? [I'm with you; I'm trying to get the feeling you have and if I'm off target you'll let me know.]

JOHNNY: (Raising his voice to a tone of frustration) *Yeah! Just because I'm in the fourth grade and they're all in the sixth. I can play as good as them.*

MOM: (Again picking up the nonverbalized feeling from the tone of his voice) *That must feel* **frustrating** *for you, especially if you know you can play as well as they*

JOHNNY: *Well, maybe not quite as good.*

MOM: *You don't?*

JOHNNY: *No. They're two years older and they've played more. When I'm in sixth grade, I'll play as good as they do.*

MOM: *I think you will, too.*

JOHNNY: *Yeah. Can I have a snack?* (Trots off)

Often, with children (and grown-ups, too) their feelings are closer to the surface than their understanding of a situation. Johnny's feelings were hurt, but through withness listening he learned *for himself* that sixth-graders want to play with sixth-graders. Above all, in so many words, he heard his mother say, "I'm really *with* you, Johnny." And the mother-son relationship is that much closer, an actual-belonging.

The primary function of checking-out is toward an *enhanced understanding* of the other person. When you're checking-out, you'll notice that sometimes the nonverbal communication of the other person is not congruent. For example, he may be chuckling at the same time that he is saying something that is not humorous. You are now in the position of either assuming what message he's really sending or else asking him what's tickling him and, conceivably, find out. Following is an example of this:

BILL: *What do you think of the new man's efficiency on the job?*

74

TOM: *Well* (chuckle), *he seems to be doing okay.* [The assumption here could be that the new man's efficiency is laughable.]

BILL: *What were you chuckling at just then, Tom?*

TOM: *Oh, I always feel nervous when I'm asked to evaluate someone.*

It's not unusual for someone not to be aware of how he is coming across to others. You can, at that moment, verbally check-out this individual's communication and let him know, *in a friendly way,* what you hear him communicating. Be clear on this. When you verbally check-out the other's communication, you do so without animosity, vindictiveness, or protest. Now what he does with this is entirely up to him. That's the end of it. If you mention it more than once at that moment, it becomes nagging.

Lill, my wife, had one such experience when she was learning to check-out:

"I was in a store buying curtains and the owner was quite gruff and abrupt with me and I hadn't done anything to provoke him. It was just his way. I said, 'You sound like you're angry with me.' He looked surprised and immediately stopped, as though suspended for a moment. And then he said, 'No, I'm not.' Directly he became different and he wasn't so irritable-sounding."

It may be clear by now that checking-out is the antithesis of introspection. The latter is involved with deep thinking, asking *why*, analyzing, making high-level inferences and interpretations. Checking-out is the sharpening of one's observational powers, and the more you practice it, the better you get at it. There is no interpreting, no analyzing *whys*. Introspection is the closing of one's eyes and ears to the world and sinking deep into a well of self-analysis. Checking-out is an opening of the eyes and ears to the world outside of the self, and tasting, even if momentarily, everything in your sphere of contact. Whether you're with a rose, a kitten, or a human, at that moment, that rose, that kitten, or that human is the center of your world. The secret of eternal depression, anxiety, or guilt is never to check-out—just introspect.

My students consistently report a curious phenomenon of checking-out. When they are checking-out, they find they *cannot* experience self-consciousness—that unpleasant feeling that is the mother of embarrassment. Perhaps this is because one is getting outside of himself and into another person's world. Instead of wondering, "How is he feeling about me?" the wondering is "How is he feeling?"

The following exchange is with Margaret Louise Orear, a retired Assistant Superintendant of Schools. It concerns a most poignant situation centering around her elderly mother.

M.L.: *Sometimes I feel so self-conscious and ill at ease around my mother. Its as though whatever I do doesn't please her. She's always complaining to me about one thing or another and it's become so unpleasant that I've cut my visits down from once a week to once every two weeks. It's really just a duty.*

DR. B.: *You're one of the most conscientious and empathetic persons I know, and I would guess you're capable of heaping lots of guilt on yourself.*

M.L.: *Oh, yes, I'm good at that.*

DR. B.: *We all go through some kind of grief reaction when a family member dies. Would you right now fantasize—you're at your mother's bedside and she has just died. Say something to her.*

M.L.: (Closing her eyes) *Mother, I—I* (tears)— *I'm sorry we weren't closer. Oh, it's so hard to do this, Dr. B.*

DR. B.: *You've just gotten a small taste of the grief reaction. I went through a long one when my mother died—too long—and I wish now I'd had someone open my eyes before she died. No matter how good a son or daughter we may be, we all feel guilt and grief when a parent dies. But the guilt can be less, and the grief reaction shorter.*

M.L.: *How?*

DR. B.: *We don't know how long your mother is going to live. We do know that how you belong with each other can be a lot better than it is now—and you can do something about it.*

M.L.: *I'd like that.*

The session continued with much instruction and practice in checking-in and checking-out with withness listening.

DR. B.: *Now, in the weeks to come, practice what you've learned here with your mother. She seems like an excellent subject.*

M.L.: *If I can do this with her, I can do it with anybody.*

DR. B.: *You'll notice your self-consciousness and tension virtually melting away when you're with her.*

For the next few months Margaret Louise reported she was experiencing the best relationship of her life with her mother. "We've never been closer and for some reason she doesn't complain like she used to." A few weeks later the mother suddenly died of a stroke. Margaret Louise had her grief reaction. It was of short duration because paramount in her mind was, "I feel so good that we got to know each other finally and that I really did something about it. She loved me and I loved her and we both knew it. It's such a good feeling." Needless to say, this was one of the more gratifying experiences I've been fortunate enough to have in this field.

Some years ago when my wife, Lill, was first learning the part of checking-out I like to call *withness listening,* she wrote down her experiences for the class work.

Unfortunately, we can't locate her original notes, but Lill has reconstructed them as well as possible. The following words are Lill's:

"This happened a number of years ago when I was studying withness listening. To the best of my recollection, it went like this: Melody, our daughter, who was about thirteen years old at the time, came home from school and flopped on her bed. When I went in to see her, she said, 'Boy, my legs hurt. The gym teacher had me run around the track twice!'

ME: (With annoyance) *I don't see why they rush you kids into those long runs around the track without gradually working up to it. Your muscles aren't ready for it. Do you want me to talk to the teacher about it?*

MELODY: (Quietly) *No.*

ME: [I left the room and realized I hadn't withness listened. So I went back into Melody's room a few minutes later and sat on the bed.] *Your legs must be really hurting.*

MELODY: *It's not really so bad.* (Silence)

ME: (Trying again) *You must have been really mad at your gym teacher.*

MELODY: *Well, the second time around the track she was having me pace another girl.* [A flicker of pride came across her face.]

ME: *You liked that?*

MELODY: *Yes, because she thought I ran real fast and I could help the other girl keep up a fast pace.*

ME: *That was kind of an honor, wasn't it?*

MELODY: *Yes.* (Smiling)

Withness listening opened the doors for Melody to express the pride she felt in herself. And I learned so much more the second time around when I withness listened. I learned that she was a good runner and that she actually felt good about this particular episode but apparently didn't know how to go about getting it across. I also learned that my anger at the teacher was out of place. Withness listening was new to me at the time, and I was glad that I had another way to communicate than my usual way."

I believe that a parent's greatest joy may be the conviction that he or she has made a worthwhile contribution in enriching the lives of his children. Melody and her high school sweetheart, Steve, have been in many of my groups at the training center. On one occasion in 1973 I asked her if she would jot down for me any experiences she had had in checking-in and checking-out. Following is an excerpt from her letter.

"*I discovered something. I was discussing something trivial with Steve not long ago, and when I checked-in at that moment, I observed how fiercely I put down a suggestion of his. I felt uncomfortable catching myself doing this, but I still did it and it took several times of checking-in for me to feel uncomfortable* enough *to want not to do it. And when I checked-out I suddenly saw that* my *feelings weren't the only reason I felt the need to change because it was obvious to me that he was feeling hurt by my manner of relating to him— funny I wasn't aware of that before.*

"*Each time I put him down I checked-in to heighten my awareness of the low self-esteem I felt at the time. After a while, I was able to catch myself in time and just stopped putting him down. And when I would check-out during these times, I could see that his feelings weren't hurt. One time I asked Steve to check-in himself after one of these dialogues and he said his self-esteem had increased—and mine had, too.*

"*Voilà! After much conscious thought and action I've developed the habit of relating to Steve in a more adult way. No longer do I put him down, but rather, I've found I can really appreciate his suggestions. What once was a difficult exercise is* natural *now.*

"*Though the two of us still have some difficulties because we compete with each other, we have come a long way. I have rid myself, by checking-in and out, of an unpleasant method of communicating with him, and therefore, in these situations, our whole manner of relating to each other has changed for the good.*"

Melody and Steve subsequently married in 1974, and I asked them about a year afterward if they had a follow-up on the '73 letter. This is the response:

"It's difficult to put into words just how much checking-in and out has affected our lives. We're much more accepting of others than before, but, more important, there's not a hint of competitiveness between us anymore. We're closer than ever and love each other more every day. Checking-in and out is part of our daily lives now."

Lill and I know that Steve and Melody are pitilessly honest and individualistic poeple and wouldn't bend the truth for any reason, so you can imagine the effect their personal experience has had on us. It's a precious moment in our lives.

Before moving on to other aspects of loving and being loved, I'll summarize the ideas and methods presented in the first four chapters. The phenomenon of *belonging* was described as a nucleus from which much of human behavior springs. I portrayed it as the kernel of virtually every form of communication, from the casual two-second hello to the warm exchange of lovers. Communicative habits of trying to manipulate others for love, acceptance, approval, or esteem I've referred to as *quasi-belonging* habits. Those habits that are not manipulative of others were called *actual-belonging* habits. I also dealt with the considerable energies expended in quasi-belonging and the minimal energies used in actual-belonging, thus freeing these energies for more constructive purposes.

The core principle of moving toward actual-belonging is *owning yourself,* and the basic techniques for

accomplishing this are *checking-in* and *checking-out*.
Every time you check-in, you may catch yourself being
98 percent with your work and 2 percent with your
family. Or you may catch yourself being 98 percent with
your children and 2 percent with your mate. Or you
may catch yourself trying to make others feel guilty. You
must catch yourself in the act before you can *own* that
behavior and do something about it. You have to catch
a chicken to eat it.

I've stressed that checking-in is a *friendly* acknowledging
of *what* you're doing and *how* you're doing it at that very
moment. You can ask yourself why if you wish, but I
don't suggest it since it's academic. Either you're going
to choose to discard the habit or you aren't, no matter how
much insight you may have.

Checking-out others (including withness listening) is an
integral part of the process of actual-belonging because it
is a mutual experience. At its core is the refreshing
message "I see you clearly. I hear you clearly. I'm aware
of you." It's hard to be loved by others without knowing
where *they* are. Checking-out is a vehicle for learning
how others are thinking, how they are feeling, how they
are communicating, and how they see the world. The
benefits of checking-out, whether verbally or nonverbally,
are considerable. They include a marked diminishing or
eliminating of self-consciousness, anxiety, and depression,
a sharpened perceptivity of the feelings and thoughts
of others, and a concomitant heightening of interest in
others. You will see more color and beauty in life, be it
plant, animal, or human. You will be getting a firsthand

report of the response of others to your person. You'll discover in others, especially when you become habituated to withness listening, and increasing interest and appreciation of you, without your manipulating for it.

To me and to most of my students, the most significant attribute of checking-out is that, as it becomes an unconscious part of your behavior, you will discover that you are accepting others' desire to belong, rather than being judgmental or scared of them. I believe that one of the reasons for this may be that when you are checking-out, you are really acknowledging that every person wants to be loved and accepted, but some have developed habits that hinder them from actual-belonging. You will particularly discover that being loved is not something you strive for as much as it is something you *are*. When you are loving, you are loved.

5

Whatever You Tell Yourself and Believe Is Then True for You

"I'm always nervous around people I don't know."

"Those kids just drive me up the wall."

"I just can't seem to have an orgasm."

"Those kind of people bug the hell out of me."

"You embarrass me whenever you do that."

85

"I just can't seem to stop smoking."

"You can't really trust anybody."

"I feel like I'm different from others somehow."

"I've had nothing but bad breaks all my life."

"I just can't get a good night's sleep."

"The pressure of this job is killing me."

"I just can't seem to hold on to a man."

"I have a terrible temper."

"I'm forever putting things off."

"I don't believe I know what love is."

THESE ARE THE STATEMENTS OF UNHAPPY PEOPLE—
people who have often been convinced by professionals
or amateurs that they are *neurotic*. I'm convinced that
this word *neurotic* is a snarl term that contributes to the
semantic muddiness of psychiatry. The term implies that
neurotics are in one box and *nonneurotics* in another.
No such separation exists—only a continuum. I don't
believe that *neurosis* or *normality* are two actual, definable
states. Rather, they can be seen as forms of the same
process. As such, they can be defined with the same
definition, as follows: *Whatever you tell yourself—and
believe—is then true for you, and you behave accordingly.*
What you believe about yourself or others paints itself
on your face, colors your intonations, and programs your
thoughts, feelings, words, and body movements. For
example, if you tell yourself that if people really knew
you, they would look down on you, and you believe that,
then, no matter how you may try to camouflage it, your

face, your eyes, and your general attitude broadcast the message "I feel inferior and self-conscious." This in turn influences how others react to you. It also influences how you are loved by others and how you are able to love them. Whether you tell yourself you're adequate or inadequate, pretty or plain, worthwhile or worthless, dependent or independent, it has a direct bearing on how you belong to your world of people. The point here is that what you tell yourself and have faith in may be the single most powerful force available to you. Consider the following laboratory demonstrations of this power.

Forty-three patients with high blood pressure were divided into two groups. The purpose of the study[2] was to evaluate the effectiveness of reducing high blood pressure by irradiating the pituitary gland at the base of the brain. The only difference between the two groups was that the X-ray machine was turned on for one group and not for the other. Both groups were told that their blood pressure would drop. Following are the results:

	X-RAY MACHINE TURNED ON	X-RAY MACHINE TURNED OFF
Patients in whom blood-pressure was lowered	68%	77.7%
Patients with "marked" decrease in blood pressure (30 points systole, 20 points diastole)	12%	16.6%

The doctor didn't lower the blood pressure. The "turned off" machine didn't lower it. The only thing that could have done it was the inner conviction of the subjects. *It's what you tell yourself and believe.*

The term *placebo,* from the Latin "I will please," can be defined as a pharmacologically inert substance, usually in pill form, such as sugar, that elicits, upon administration, certain physiological and psychological effects that cannot be explained on a pharmacological baisis—hence the name *sugar pill.*

Seventeen patients suffering from bleeding ulcers were divided into two groups.[3] One group was told, "You are to be given a medicine that, without any doubt, will give you *prompt relief."* The "medicine" (placebo) was then administered by *physicians.* The second group was told, "You are to be given a medicine that is in the *experimental stage,* and its effects are more or less unknown." This "medicine" (also a placebo) was administered by *nurses.* The results follow:

DRUG	ADMINISTERED BY	PATIENTS RELIEVED
placebo	physician	70%
placebo	nurse	20%

The purpose of the study was to see what effect, if any, the giving of a supposed medicine by a higher and more positive-speaking authority has on the outcome of "treatment" for bleeding ulcers. Ostensibly, it would appear that the individual's faith in the authority and in the words of the authority play a more important role than his faith in the medicine. *It's what you tell yourself and believe.*

Another demonstration of the power of faith is seen in the "voodoo curse." An individual believes he has been bewitched or that he has transgressed a taboo and abruptly dies without discernible organic cause. Literature is replete with case histories documented by anthropologists and other social scientists. Here is a typical case:[4] "A sorcerer in New Guinea had been offended by a young Papuan. In revenge he told the young, healthy man that a few days ago he [the sorcerer] had put a 'bofiet' (an object poisoned by witchcraft) into the young man's path. The young Papuan immediately became extremely ill and within two days he was dead. The sorcerer was indicted by a Dutch court which, recognizing the bewitchment as cause of death, condemned the sorcerer—who, by the way, admitted his guilt freely—to several years of imprisonment."

That which is puzzling to the scientists studying "voodoo death" is not that it happens, but that it happens so frequently. A further note of interest is that when the point of death is almost reached and the voodoo is lifted, the condemned ones "return to life."

Death resulting from death expectancy, or the *will to die,* is not unknown in the Western world, but death resulting from a curse (with the exception of a physician's pronouncement that a person has only six months to live) is not popular here. The occasional patient who is given six months to live and then proceeds to frustrate the pronouncing physician by living on year after year because of his *will to live* demonstrates the power of *what you tell yourself and believe.*

A lesser known phenomenon is that called *koro*[5], a phobia experienced among the Bugi and the Macassarese in Celebes and West Borneo. In China the condition is given the name of *shook-yong*. The basis of the phobia is the individual's belief that his penis will disappear into his abdomen and that he will die. To prevent this, he grips his penis firmly, and when he gets tired, his wife, relatives, and friends lend a hand. The Chinese also have a special wooden clasp constructed for this purpose. Fellatio, applied immediately by the individual's wife, has been known to lift the victim's spirits and to end the phobia. Some have been accused of feigning *shook-yong* in order to receive the treatment. Perhaps a Western equivalent of this phobia is that which is referred to in the psychoanalytic literature as "castration fear." No matter, the principle again obtains—*it's what you tell yourself and believe.*

One final illustration of this power of thought or faith is seen in "hypnosis." I place quotes around the word, since I believe it can be misleading. Derived from "Hypnos," the Greek god of sleep, the implication is that when you are under hypnosis you are asleep and someone is doing something to you. This is not the case. Electroencephalic studies[6-7] reveal that the brain wave patterns in hypnosis subjects are consistent with the *alert* state, not the *sleep* state. Academicians have documented that no "hypnotist" can "hypnotize" anyone who does not *choose* to become "hypnotized." A more accurate description of the process would be "self-induction, with or without an *instructor*."

There are many fables about self-induction (hypnosis). The process has been referred to as dangerous, mysterious, unnatural, and that it can induce the subject to lose his willpower, etc. I believe that self-induction is as old as life. It is natural, pleasant, easy to learn, utterly safe, and most relaxing. It is a manifestation of the simple utilization of *unconscious power* and is practiced by four-legged as well as two-legged animals. When the bear hibernates, slowing his metabolic processes to the point that he virtually suspends digestion and defecation, he is practicing self-induction. This hibernation process is not an exclusive franchise of the bear. Frogs, fish, reptiles, horseshoe crabs, snails, hummingbirds, insects, arachnids—all can induce a trancelike or dormant state at appropriate times. Some trees, plants, seeds, winter eggs of sponges, and Polyzoa also have their dormant stages. When the alligator, an air-breathing reptile, stays motionless underwater for two days, he has slowed his metabolic processes to such an extent that his vital signs (blood pressure, heart rate, respiration) cannot be measured. The deer in the forest practices self-induction when she "freezes." The predator only twenty feet away cannot pick up the scent of the deer because the chemistry producing it has been almost totally suspended. The meditating yogi who stays ten hours in an airtight chamber with only one hour of available oxygen to sustain life at the ordinary metabolic rate is practicing self-induction. Like the hibernating animals he also has slowed down his cardiovascular and respiratory systems. We practice unintentional self-induction daily. That twilight zone just prior to falling asleep or awakening is self-induction. Intentional self-induction involves shutting out external stimuli by concentrating on a single word, idea, or object. The process is similar to blushing at a faux pas or "getting sick at the sight of blood" or being so engrossed in a book that you don't "hear" your name called.

If you would enjoy a demonstration of your own power of self-induction right now, perform this brief exercise. Settle comfortably in your chair or bed. Place your hands, palms up, on your lap or at your sides. Let all your muscles go limp, including the jaw and facial muscles. Now focus all your attention on the following word: *tingling*—tingling in the hands or feet, the same "pins and needles" sensation as when they "fall asleep." You'll be better able to concentrate on this word if you close your eyes. Concentrate on *tingling* in the tips of the fingers. Within sixty seconds, as you notice the sensation in the tips of your fingers, gradually increase the sensation down your fingers toward the palms of your hands. Go ahead—I'll wait for you. The instant you move your fingers, the tingling disappears.

The only way you were able to produce this temporary tingling sensation was by voluntarily controlling the so-called involuntary peripheral nervous system. *It's what you tell yourself and believe.*

Each of the foregoing demonstrations depended upon the fact that each of the subjects relies on something or someone much as he might have relied on his mother earlier in life. In other circumstances, any one of the subjects may demonstrate this kind of *faith* in prayers to

Allah, or in a witch doctor, a hygienic system, a religious science, fasting, faith healing, sunbathing, a psychiatrist, acupuncture, yogurt, "getting into an experience," tarot cards, astrology, a father, or himself. "Is any sick among you? let him call the elders of the church; and let them pray over him, anointing him with oil in the name of the Lord. And the prayer of faith shall save the sick and the Lord shall raise him up" (James 5:14). Possibly "Lord," in this passage, represents not only the "Lord" *over* each of us, but also the "Lord" *in** each of us—that essence of the power of faith, of belief in ourselves, that is always there, waiting to be called upon. The witch doctor, the faith healer, the placebo, the psychiatrist, the hypnotist, are *powerless without the power of the believer.* The question here is how to awaken the believer—that's you— to the reality that *you-are-the-power,* that you literally, moment by moment, are pointing yourself in the direction of your choosing. The following session illustrates the awakening process of a student as he gradually and reluctantly faces the fact that he is the ultimate responsible source of how he thinks, feels, and communicates.

FRANK: (Very serious expression) *My problem is that I just can't seem to make decisions.*

DR. B.: *Do you believe that?*

FRANK: *Yes, I do.*

DR. B.: *Then that's true for you. That's your choice and you'll continue to behave as if you "can't" make decisions.*

---

* See Ephesians 4:6.

FRANK: *What do you mean, "as if"? I don't make decisions.*

DR. B.: *Now, that's different. Which do you believe, Frank—that you* can't *make decisions or that you* don't *make decisions?*

FRANK: *I don't, I guess—well, I can't. Oh, I don't know which it is.*

DR. B.: Can't *implies the idea of something being hopeless or impossible. Now, Frank, if you were to say to me, "I* can't *have a baby," I'd listen more attentively to that.*

FRANK: (Reluctantly) *Okay, so I don't make decisions.*

DR. B.: *Maybe we're closer to the truth when we say, "You are making decisions all the time. Right* now *you're deciding to be undecided. And if you would acknowledge, that is, own where you are right now without the serious show of a struggle, you'd be ahead of the game.*

FRANK: (Chuckling) *That sounds funny—I'm deciding to be undecided.*

DR. B.: *Yeah, it does, doesn't it? Reality is often funny.*

FRANK: *But I don't want to be undecided.*

DR. B.: *Believe what you do, Frank, not what you say. You do what you choose all the time, whether it's conscious or unconscious.*

FRANK: *You mean maybe I* want *to be undecided?*

DR. B.: *In some things, maybe—not in all. You're selective in what you choose to be undecided about. For example, I think you make the decision whether to defecate in the living room or in the bathroom. If you didn't, that would be an exquisite indecision—a completely unique indecision.* (Dr. B. straining as if to defecate while holding his chin in perplexion and looking around as though trying to decide where to do it)

FRANK: (Laughing) *I don't think you're taking me seriously.*

DR. B.: *I'm focusing on your power, and you're focusing on your way of making yourself look powerless. Sometimes I think the best medicine in the world is to take yourself with a grain of salt. The Tahitians have a phrase for it, "Aita pea pea." It sums up their philosophy of life—"No sweat."*

FRANK: *Yeah, that's my problem, too. I take myself too seriously.*

DR. B.: *Do you believe that that's a "problem," Frank?*

FRANK: *Yeah.*

DR. B.: *Then that's true for you, too. And if some ingrate came around and stole that "problem" from you, you'd run around like mad until you found another "problem" you could settle down with.*

FRANK: *I don't understand. Isn't it a problem, I mean, when I take myself seriously like that?*

DR. B.: *No, it's a habit you have right now, and you can give it the name "problem" if you wish, Frank. What I'm suggesting is that so-called problems aren't*

*significant by themselves. They'll always exist. Take
one away and another pops up. That's what life is made
up of—problems. It's what you tell yourself, that is,
your attitude toward the problems, that is significant.
Your choice is whether you're going to make a big deal
of them or just deal with them.*

FRANK: *Okay—so what would you call it when I take
myself seriously or when I'm indecisive, if it isn't a
problem?*

DR. B.: *It's a habit—it's a psychological clothing you
wear to carry you through life.*

FRANK: *But I don't do that on purpose.*

DR. B.: *Whether it's conscious or unconscious, it's still
you who is doing the choosing. I invite you to own
yourself, Frank.*

FRANK: (Very serious, almost dramatic) *Why in God's
name would I choose to be so serious or not make
decisions?*

DR. B.: *Maybe that's the way you've learned to belong to
others. By being indecisive, you can attract someone
else to come along and make decisions for you.*

FRANK: *And you think I'm manipulating people with
my seriousness, too?*

DR. B.: *Yes, but you don't plan it. It's unconscious. You
want to belong, to be accepted like anyone else, and
when you're very serious about yourself, like now,
you're inviting me to take you very seriously, too.*

FRANK: *You mean I shouldn't take myself so seriously.*

DR. B.: *If I said, "Stop taking yourself so seriously and stop being indecisive," do you think you'd do it?*

FRANK: (Looking down and smiling to himself)

DR. B.: *Give the smile a voice, Frank.*

FRANK: *Well, the smile is saying—I'm embarrassed to say it—"I already had reasons why I should be serious if you'd said I shouldn't be."*

DR. B.: *Great.*

FRANK: *What's great about that?*

DR. B.: *You just checked-in to how you're belonging to me right now.*

FRANK: *How?*

DR. B.: *As the friendly guru confounder. It's like a Ping-Pong game. I'll tell you why you shouldn't be serious and you tell me why you should.*

FRANK: *Okay—but what's the answer?*

DR. B.: *I can't decide. It's too serious.*

FRANK: (Laughing)

DR. B.: (Laughing, caught up in Frank's reaction)

FRANK: *I just decided something* (laughing). *You're a sonofabitch.*

DR. B.: (Laughing) *Thank you, Frank. That's the nicest thing you said to me today. It's so light and spontaneous. But we have a new "problem."*

FRANK: *What's that?* (Still smiling, most unserious, mischievous expression on his face)

DR. B.: *The problem of* not *taking yourself very seriously and not being indecisive right now. Check-in. Where are you?*

FRANK: *My shoulders feel light—like something is taken off. I feel lifted. I certainly don't feel very serious about myself.*

DR. B.: *Are you sure of that? No indecision about that?*

FRANK: *Right!*

DR. B.: *Then that's true for you right now and you'll behave accordingly.*

The function of this chapter has been to give you a clearer perspective of the power you may never have known you had and of the ultimate responsibility you do have for how you choose to use that power. The key to releasing this power is a simple, honest *acknowledging* to yourself that *you really do own this power*—that you really are responsible for how you choose to treat others or yourself. There are no shortcuts or tapping your power. It isn't simply a matter of declaring, "I'm going to be a better person now" or "I'm going to be a positive thinker now" or "I'm going to be a violin player now." It takes practice, repeatedly checking-in, catching yourself in the act of being superserious or indecisive or whatever, and checking-out, getting outside yourself and into the fascinating panorama of the life of others.

This letter from William E. Neuhauser, a Long Beach executive and student of the training center, may clarify what I've been saying in the last few chapters (the Roman type is mine):

"I'm not sure that I made clear the point I was trying to get across in our discussion the other day, so I'm going to try again, this time in writing.

As you've observed many times, I've got some pretty fixed ideas on how people 'should' look, act, talk, etc., and when I'm exposed to people who don't conform to these preconceived ideas, I turn them off, or as you might put it, my impatience shows through. This makes establishing satisfactory relationships difficult.

You've stressed the process of checking-in and checking-out in relating to other people. I've tried hard in practicing these techniques and I think I've become pretty good at checking-out. I have a hard time, however, getting in touch with my own feelings and thus, being able to own them. So in relating to people who, for one reason or another, turn me off, I found myself doing a good job checking-out on them, but I still wanted to turn them off and no amount of checking-in changed my reaction. I became aware of what I was doing, but I still did it.

Lately, I've been breaking out of this rut, and the way I've done it is to tell myself, when I am exposed to a person who I find hard to take for some reason or another, that, after all, whatever mannerism they are exhibiting is nothing more than a style which they have adopted to gain acceptance from me and the other people in this world. Now that I believe this, I can accept the behavior pattern without having feelings of disapproval, rejection, anger, or what-have-you.

99

Thus, realizing and repeating to myself that whatever image a person is projecting is simply a method used to gain acceptance is a bit of a magic formula as far as I'm concerned in enabling me to become more accepting of other people."

Bill Neuhauser's first step was to *check-in* and *own* his habit of routinely being judgmental and impatient with people. His next step was to *check-out* the multivaried habits of others when communicating face to face with him. Finally, he *told himself and believed* that their behavior "is just a style of gaining acceptance from me and the other people of the world" and that expending his energies being judgmental of people who are only trying to belong made no sense at all. This resulted in his determination to discard this useless habit and become more accepting of others.*

Irwin Rubin, M.D., is a psychoanalytically trained psychiatrist who was in one of my groups for about a year and a half. He presently is in private practice in Los Angeles and is teaching psychiatry on the staff of the USC Medical Center. I asked him to write of his personal experiences while in group for two reasons. First, I wanted the reader to see that individuals from all walks of life, including psychiatrists, have thoughts and feelings just like the reader when it comes to belonging. Secondly, knowing of his insistence on honesty, I was reasonably assured that he would not embellish the truth. Following is an excerpt from his letter:

* Feedback from Bill's group and from his wife confirms that Bill is more alive, peaceful, and accepting and loving of others. As a result he is more loved by others than at any time previously.

"The most important assumption that I recognized in group was my belief that people wouldn't like me. In your words, I 'told myself people would not like me.' I discovered that much of my time was spent trying to look good in front of others; as a result I was very self-conscious, stilted, and extremely aware of my success or failure in being liked. I was continually observing other people's responses to me. The surprise for me was to discover that people knew what I was trying to do better than I did; that is, how I was trying to get others to approve of me.

Checking-in helped me become aware of my negative self-assumption, because when I really looked at other people I saw nothing to be afraid of. I just saw people who wanted to be liked themselves. By experiencing alternate ways of looking at people in and out of group sessions, I felt a significant and pleasant emotional change towards more self-confidence. What I tell myself now is 'If I am not perfect (and who is?), so what. One cannot be any different at that moment anyway, and one can improve the next moment.'

It is gratifying to feel more comfortable with others, and to not worry so much about whether I should behave in a certain way in order to be liked. It is also gratifying to hear people who have known me for a long time say that it is more comfortable for them to be with me now. I sense that I am appreciated more now than I ever was, and the paradox of this is that I am not trying to get people to do this."

6
Your Words Mold You

WE'RE FAMILIAR WITH THE POWERFUL, IMPOSING
names of institutions such as:

> The First Security National Bank
>
> The First Congregational Church
>
> The Great Northern Railroad
>
> The Citadel Lawn Mortuary
>
> The Transcontinental Airlines

We're also conscious of other institutions with names
that attempt to convey the image of friendliness or of
being "down to earth." These places have such names as:

Bud's Hot Dog Stand

Whiz Plumbers

Manford's Holiday Motel

Frankie and Johnny's Bar and Grill

Hole in the Wall Café

Now switch some of the names of these institutions. Use imposing names for some "down to earth" names:

The First Congregational Plumbers

Whiz Airlines

Frankie and Johnny's Bank

The First Security National Hot Dog Stand

Hole in the Wall Mortuary

If these sound ludicrous* to you, then you have some inkling of how you've been conditioned by the words of others. A word is to an idea as a map is to a territory.[8] Just as the map is a representation of the territory (not the territory itself), so a word is a representation of an idea (not the idea itself). There are some maps for which there is no territory and vice versa. The point of this analogy is that a big imposing word is not a big imposing thing. It's just a symbol of something that may or may not be big and imposing. A "down to earth" word is not a "down to earth" thing. It's just a "down to earth" word. Despite the fact that a word is not an idea, the majority of us routinely confuse the two. If this were not true,

---

* I first heard this word-switching routine about five years ago as delivered by humorist George Carlin.

advertising agencies and some politicians would have been out of business long ago.

Some of us have had the misfortune to be at the receiving end of words from family members such as, "You're so stupid" or "You'll never amount to anything" or "You never seem to learn." We've often confused the words with the idea that we actually *are* stupid or will never *actually* amount to anything or *actually* will never learn. By having these words driven home repeatedly, many have been so conditioned that some have *actually* fulfilled the prophecy.

When you face the power of others' words upon you, you can also face the power your words have on others. You then realize the responsibility you have in choosing your words and how, through repetition, they are conditioning others. This responsibility is especially apparent in relation to children. You can choose words that are sarcastic, objective, supportive, judgmental, exaggerating, honest, or dishonest. In any case your words are constantly molding or structuring the personality of your child. This is done in two ways: (1) by conditioning him to believe that the words you use describe him as he actually is, and (2) by conditioning him to adopt your words with the consequent development of certain attitudes and behavior. You are a model and molder of your child's behavior.

Most of you were already aware that the repeated words of others can condition or mold you just as your words, oft repeated, can condition and mold others. What is not as well known is *how your own words can mold you.*

To clarify this boomerang effect of your words, it is essential to understand the conditioning that produces it.

Repetition is an essential part of this conditioning process. The more frequently you repeat a process, be it cigarette smoking or cigarette nonsmoking, the more you are conditioning yourself. That is, you are making it easier to smoke or not to smoke. This principle applies to anything you do, including *repeatedly* using certain words as part of your vocabulary.

Each culture finds words for things which that culture values, and these words then reinforce those values. Eskimos have twenty words for snow. The Aborigines have forty words for various family relationships, and our language has twenty. You can't ask in Chinese, "Will you answer me yes or no?" because there aren't any words for "yes" or "no" in Chinese. You couldn't ask a Hopi Indian, in his tongue, where he was, where he is, or where he will be, because time is nonsegmented in this language—no past, present, or future. For the Hopi, time just goes on and the river deeps, the leaf greens, and the tree talls.

Like a sculptor's chisel, the language of a culture shapes the form of that culture's logic, attitudes, and perceptions. You can experience this phenomenon for yourself right now. Try, if you can, for even a moment, to live in the Hopi's timeless, flowing world. You wouldn't be able to say, "I *am* here *now.*" It seems inconceivable, doesn't it? However, the Hopi's nonsegmented time is not inconceivable or illogical. It is just a manifestation of the ineptitude of our language in providing us with the conceptual tools to encompass the logic of nonsegmented time.

In the Spanish language, if you were to accidentally break a vase, you would say, *"El vaso se me quebro."* Translated, this means, "The vase broke on me." What interests me about this is that the language gives the vase life, as though it has the ability to break itself, thus ostensibly reducing the responsibility of the actual breaker. In the English language there can be a similar unconscious molding of irresponsibility. For example, it is sanctioned usage to say, "I am enjoying myself." It is not sanctioned usage to say, "I am frustrating myself." Rather, the term "frustrate" is almost always used to point the finger of blame at someone or something else. "He frustrates me." "That frustrated me." It appears that our language has a built-in escape hatch that permits us to duck out of our accountability when we are faced with a more seedy side of our behavior.

"She made me mad." "He made me cry." "They make me self-conscious." For me, a more compelling logic is that no one has the power to *make* you frustrated, or *make* you lose your temper, or *make* you cry, or *make* you self-conscious without your total cooperation. No one has that power but you.

Now I invite you to go one step further with me. My conviction is that it is not only the words and syntax that we use as a member of the culture which molds us. It is also the words and syntax we choose as a free agent within the culture that also conditions us. Consider the following words:

"Phony!"

"Sonofabitch!"

"Whore!"

"Crybaby!"

"Honkey!"

"Jerk!"

"Pig!"

"Fag!"

"Nigger!"

"Goy!"

"Snob!"

"Bastard!"

"Brat!"

"Stupid!"

These words are referred to as "snarl"[9] terms. The boomerang effect of snarl terms means that the individual who is the receiver of the snarl term is not the only one being damaged. The one sending it, the snarler, is also damaging himself, but the nature of the damage is insidious, deeper, and more permanent. I am not suggesting that the dictionary definition of the words is the only conditioning influence molding him. I am suggesting also that his own *conscious or unconscious intent to hurt* with words is also molding him as he utters them. These words from his mouth are like strokes of a whip. The reinforcer (reward) for hurling snarl terms at another may be, like after whipping someone, the tension relief that the snarler experiences. This reinforcer (tension relief) may then serve to further condition him to repeat these words whenever tension builds up again. A habit is being developed with each such use.

The very first time you call someone a "phony" or a "sonofabitch" it's a little hard to do. It's like inhaling on a cigarette for the first time. The second time it isn't quite so difficult, and about the fiftieth time it may seem that this intent to hurt someone is becoming an addiction— and it is. It's as though you are planting seeds of poison in your system and harvesting what you seed at the moment of planting. Conversely, when you repeatedly choose to utter words that are objective, fair, and accepting, and your intent is genuine, you are simultaneously, unconsciously experiencing the nourishing effect of that choice. You are planting seeds of respect from yourself and from others. You harvest whatever you seed.

I've used "snarl" terms as an example of how sheer repetition can condition or mold your personality because it's easy to grasp the validity of this example. The principle, however, is applicable to any words or syntax you *repeatedly* choose to use. The following excerpt from a session will clarify this idea:

DR. B.: *Where are you right now, Mary? Will you check-in?*

MARY: *Oh, I don't know. I'm kind of wondering what you're thinking.*

DR. B.: *"Kind of wondering"—is that like "not quite wondering"?*

MARY: *Well, I am wondering what's going to happen. I'm not saying you should tell me, but it is sort of hard to know—uh—what's going to happen.*

DR. B.: *"Sort of hard"—does that mean "not really hard"?*

MARY: *It is hard. I don't know why I say "sort of."*

DR. B.: *"Sort of" and "kind of" are words you use habitually, Mary. When you use them, it's hard to know exactly where you stand. It's a habit.*

MARY: *Yeah, it's not very definite, is it? I guess I'd like to drop that habit.*

DR. B.: *You're not sure you'd like to drop it?*

MARY: *Yes—(laughs)—I did it again, didn't I? I definitely, positively want to drop it. (Laughs) Can you help me definitely? (Mischievous expression)*

DR. B.: *I sort of feel I can kind of help somewhat maybe.*

MARY: (Laughing) *There's lots of words like that. I wonder if I—are there any others?*

DR. B.: *The most popular are "sort of," "kind of," "I guess," "rather," "maybe," "up to a point," "somewhat," "in a way," "to a certain extent," and "perhaps." I like to call all these "vaguerizers" since they make your unique identity more and more vague both to yourself and to others. The extra message is: "I'm a moving target and you can't reject someone if you don't know where they stand on anything. This is sort of, kind of, in a way, me.*

MARY: *I much prefer to let you know where I stand.*

DR. B.: *Like right now?*

MARY: *Yes. But I'm deliberately—I mean I'm doing it on purpose—not saying the sort of's.*

DR. B.: *Consciously. You're checking-in.*

MARY: *Yes.*

DR. B.: *And after a while it'll be unconscious. You'll be so much in the habit of communicating in a definite way that it will be part of your personality. It's a more honest way of communicating. You're taking more responsibility for what you're saying.*

Mary wants to belong, to be accepted, but it's as though she is saying, "I'm afraid to let you see exactly who I am. I'm afraid to risk your disagreeing or disapproving of me so this is 'sort of' me." And each time Mary uses a vaguerizer she's conditioning herself to use it again and again, making herself more and more vague. Each time she chooses *not* to use a vaguerizer she's conditioning herself to not use it again and again, and uncovering the unique individual she's always been. She's undergoing a process of unlearning.

I want to remind the reader once more that thinking, feeling, and communicating are intimately related. Modify any one of the three and the other two are affected. Mary was not born with vaguerizers. When, as a baby, she felt uncomfortable, she let others know exactly how she felt, clearly and distinctly, without vaguerizers or any other show of insecurity. As she grew older she learned words and groupings of words that, by repetition, acted like an umbrella under which to hide her feelings and thoughts. Now she is learning that she can communicate in a more secure way. Repeatedly communicating in this more secure way affects how she thinks and feels, especially in regard to self-confidence. This, in turn, attracts people who want to know where where she stands.

When Tricia attends to what she is communicating, she discovers she's living in a world of *shoulds.* Again and again she hears herself saying, *should,* or one of its substitutes such as *ought, must, got to, have to,* or *supposed to.* Here is an excerpt from one of her sessions:

TRICIA: *I know that screaming and insulting kids is not the way to go. I know I shouldn't do that.*

DR. B.: *Oh, I see. But you still do it?*

TRICIA: *Yes. I find I continue to do it even though the best of—my intention—I don't want to do it.*

DR. B.: *Oh—*

TRICIA: *And I feel badly about it. I know I shouldn't and I don't want to scream at them.*

DR. B.: *Believe what you do, Tricia—not what you say. When you scream, you want to scream.*

TRICIA: *Yeah, but I don't want to scream at them.*

DR. B.: *Don't believe what you tell me now. Believe what you do.*

TRICIA: *I scream. Yes, I screamed and I said things that I* shouldn't *say.*

DR. B.: *So long as you choose to say things that you* shouldn't *say, you'll always be saying things that you* shouldn't *say. You always say what you want to say and you always do what you want to do.*

TRICIA: Want?

DR. B.: *Yes. In my dictionary, to want to, to will to, to choose to, are synonymous. They mean the same thing for me. Now—*

TRICIA: *This is—uh—"want" is—I don't quite understand.*

DR. B.: *If I say to you, "I really don't want to put this watch on but I'm afraid I'll forget it." (Dr. B. puts watch on), it isn't true. I put my watch on because I want to put it on, no matter what I say. No matter what I'm saying I'm always doing what I will to do. When you yell at the kids, it's because you want to yell at them. When you don't, it's because you don't want to.*

TRICIA: *So I should* believe very deeply. *I should* convince myself that I don't want to do it.

DR. B.: *Tricia, you "shiould" on yourself.*

TRICIA: *I—you said—it sounded like you said—what did you say?*

DR. B.: *I just said that you "shiould" on yourself again. It's a condensing of two words.*

TRICIA: *I thought that's what you said.* (Chuckle) *So* I shouldn't *say—there, I'm doing it again.*

DR. B.: *Fine. You're checking-in. You can check-in when you're with your children and be very aware of what you're doing while you're doing it. Check-in while you're yelling at them and listen to yourself. If it were possible to get a mirror and see your face at that time, that would help. That would be even better, but a little difficult.*

TRICIA: *No, but it isn't difficult. The kids tell me that— "Mother, your—uh—your—the ugly face is coming up."*

DR. B.: *Right.*

TRICIA: *Y'know, now—I—if they see me they tell me, "Mother, now listen, we have—now don't put up your ugly face"—and that snaps me out of it and I realize what I'm doing.*

DR. B.: *So you don't need a mirror. They invite you to check-in. Actually they're checking-out, aren't they?*

It's important to bear in mind that as long as you are saying, "I should do this or that," you aren't doing it. Try an experiment. Say to yourself, "I shouldn't [fill in your favorite sin or vice]." Now make the same statement but substitute, "I choose to . . ." or "I choose not to . . . ," whichever is accurate. Notice that you can say, "I shouldn't do this or that" and still save face while doing it. It's like you're saying, "I know I *shouldn't* do it, but at least I'm acknowledging I'm a sinner or I'm weak, so I'm not all bad and I'll be saved despite my sins, anyway." However, the moment you say, "I choose to do this or that" or "I choose not to do this or that, then you are taking *full* responsibility for your communication and your behavior. Above all, you are no longer kidding yourself or trying to kid others. It's in this sense that *shoulds are responsibility-reducers.*

Dick, another student, especially "shioulds" on himself when he is making a decision. His "shoulds" are sending the message, "No one can hold me accountable for any decision that issues from me, since the decision is really not mine. It's the decision of my 'shoulds.' " What Dick is saying is that his "should" is the equivalent of law, duty, or morality. Dick's extra message is, "If you disagree, you have to disagree with my duty, not me. I have no choice." "If you blame, you have to blame the law, not me, I have no choice." "If you disapprove, you have to disapprove of morality, not me. I have no choice." If Dick decided to own himself, he would not say, "I should be a better father" or "I have to obey this law." He would communicate about a law he didn't care about as follows: "This law is inconvenient for me. I'd prefer to not follow it, but I choose to obey it for any number of reasons, such as not wanting to be punished or wanting to follow the rules of society." Thus Dick would not be kidding himself as though he had no choice. His actual-belonging words are, "I don't have to obey this law. I choose to."

The important aspect of all this is that Dick, by checking-in, can become aware of and own his words and his behavior as his choice, his want. It's not what he *should* do that is the cause of his behavior. It's that he, Dick, chooses to do this or that. He can behave as his own autonomous person. Incidentally, the autonomous (self-directing) person is sometimes confused with the nonconformist. The truly autonomous person may conform or not conform, but he *knows* he's doing it and owns his behavior and communicates accordingly.

When Joe and Jane check-in, they will become aware that their communication system is filled with *you know?, know what I mean?, right?,* or an almost incessant head nodding while talking.

JOE: *—like this morning—sometimes she lets the baby cry and—until I'm awake, and then I get up and I get pissed off and I say, "Dammit, now I'm awake. Now are you happy?" Y'know, and now she's taking care of him but it's pissed me off, y'know, because now I can't go back to sleep. You know what I mean?—because my sleep is ruined and hers is ruined.*

DR. B.: (Jane is smiling.) *What tickles you now, Jane?*

JANE: (Chuckles) *I don't see how—I don't let him cry until he's awake. It's just that he's crying and he's not stopping. Y'know, you can't bag him and stop him from crying. Right?* (Nods head)

JOE: *Maybe she—she's not doing it intentionally, y'know, but I mean he's crying and I'm awake and she's taking care of him but, y'know, he's still crying and everything.*

JANE: (Smiling again) *I think in a way Joe is more neurotic about him in some ways—like if we go out, we'll go out, we'll be out three hours but while we're out three hours he's afraid that, y'know, that the baby is not getting along with the baby-sitter and we have to rush right back, y'know.* (Nods her head during dialogue)

DR. B.: *He's quite protective, would you say?*

JANE: (Smiling again) *Yes.*

DR. B.: *"Protective" is less of a snarl term than "neurotic," isn't it?*

JANE: *Yes, I guess.* (Chuckles again)

JOE: *I—I'm that way—uh—with him, y'know.*

DR. B.: *No, I didn't know that.*

JOE: *Oh, I didn't mean—I mean—uh, I'm that way with him.*

DR. B.: *Joe, I see that you're holding and feeding the baby right now. Do you do that at home, too?*

JOE: *Yes, probably more than Jane does.*

DR. B.: *So, in this one area, you're more of the mother and Jane's more of the—*

JANE: *—father.* (Chuckles) *Yeah.*

JOE: *It is true, y'know, because, y'know, she's more of the disciplinarian, y'know—not that I let him get away with things, y'know.*

DR. B.: *Disciplinarian?*

JOE: *Well, I mean, y'know.*

DR. B.: *Three months old and he needs a disciplinarian?*

JOE: *Well, I mean—y'know—like, I know why you're crying, y'know, this and that, or something. Whereas, don't worry, let him cry, y'know—whereas I'll go and I'll say I can't stand him crying. I'll pick him up, y'know.*

DR. B.: *No, I didn't know that.*

JOE: *I mean—uh, that's right—you don't know that. I don't know why I say that.*

DR. B.: *It's just a habit you picked up someplace. The extra message is, "Support me. Agree with me. Accept what I'm saying." It's a request of support or for reassurance from whomever you're talking with. It's as though you have a big sign on your chest that says, "I am insecure."*

Each time Joe sends his *y'know* message and is rewarded with an affirmation (a nod or a yes) by the other person, he is demonstrating the principle of *operant conditioning.* The nod or yes of the other person is reinforcing him to use "y'know" again and again. And with each "y'know" he is self-conditioning his support-seeking, quasi-belonging self at the sacrifice of his unique, assertive, responsible self. Jane's major support-seeker is the affirmative nodding of her head whenever she is talking. This support-seeking habit is probably the most demanding of them all, virtually pressuring the listener into agreement. Both Jane and Joe, through checking-in, can get introduced to these manipulative habits and discover, happily, that if they choose to discard them no substitute is required. They can also discover, by checking-in, that they do not attract people to them when they are trying to coerce these people into agreement or acceptance of whatever they are saying. Finally, as Joe or Jane is checking-in and gradually dropping this support-seeking habit of communication, each will discover that he didn't need the support in the first place and that he is molding himself to stand on his own two feet and feel all the better for it.

Dan is speaking to a friend. I'd like you, the reader, to try to uncover his quasi-belonging word habit:

"When you think of the fact that nutrition has a lot to do with our health, and then when you realize that medical schools, the watchdogs of health, don't teach nutrition to the doctors, you feel confused. And when you think of nutrition, you think of milk. When you consider that, of the four thousand or so mammals in existence, the human mammal is the only one that drinks milk after the weaning period, you wonder about that. Another thing is that, if you look at the curd, cow's milk forms a large, tough curd while human milk forms a soft,

small, flocculent mass, which is especially designed for baby's digestion. And if you compare the protein and calcium content of the two, you learn that cow's milk is over twice as great as mother's milk. And you know that makes sense, since a baby doubles its birth weight in 190 days and calf in 47 days. So you could say that cow's milk is the perfect food for baby calves and was never intended for baby humans. But then, if mothers can't produce milk, what are you going to do? You have to substitute. Anyway, I suppose you could say that the dairy industry is an essential part of our system and it does provide a lot of jobs for people."

Did you find it? Dan's quasi-belonging word is the pronoun *you*. He habitually substitutes *you* for the appropriate pronoun *I*. His extra message is, You must accept what I'm saying because we're in this together. It's not *I* who is rendering this opinion or having this feeling, it's *you*. You are responsible for these words. You can also see how modest I am.

Dan is quasi-belonging with his listener, communicating as though whoever is listening is in consort with the thought he's expressing.

Each time Dan substitutes an inappropriate *you* for an *I*, he is reinforcing the likelihood that he will substitute it again. He is simultaneously substituting a mask of generality for his special, unrepeated identity, melding himself with anyone within earshot.

If, after checking-in and discovering this word habit, Dan decided to discard it, he would sound like this:

*"When I think of the fact that nutrition has a lot to do
with health, and then when I realize that medical
schools, the watchdogs of health, don't teach
nutrition to the doctors, I feel confused. And when I
think of nutrition, I think of milk. And when I
consider that, of the four thousand or so mammals in
existence, the human mammal is the only one that
drinks milk after the weaning period, I wonder about
that. I'm aware that cow's milk forms a large, tough
curd while human milk forms a soft, small, flocculent
mass, which is especially designed for baby's digestion.
Also, the protein and calcium content of cow's milk
is over twice as great as mother's milk. And that makes
sense to me, since a baby doubles its birth weight in
190 days and a calf in 47 days. So I'm convinced that
cow's milk is the perfect food for baby calves and was
never intended for baby humans. But then, if mothers
can't produce milk, some substitute is necessary.
Anyway, I suppose the dairy industry is an essential part
of our system and it does provide a lot of jobs for people."*

In this piece of communication, Dan takes full
accountability for what he is saying instead of adroitly
trying to shift the responsibility to the listener. It's as
though he is saying, "You may or may not approve of this
thought of mine, but my integrity is more valuable to
me than your approval of me." As he repeatedly uses
words that are a more honest representation of himself
and he gets into the habit of communicating more
honestly, his way of thinking is affected. His words are
literally molding him to become more honest.

Harold is speaking. See if you can recognize his quasi-belonging phrases:

"It's generally understood that the primary problem in sex education is that the right people aren't getting together. The schools, as you're well aware, offer sex education with the idea of reducing tension about sex among the students. And, of course, the moralists are interested in maintaining some tension about sex, since, without any tension here, morals naturally become looser. Clearly, one would have to conclude that the real problem has to do with tension versus nontension. Then, of course, when the president's commission studies the problem, it focuses on rape and things like that and they don't even deal with the tension versus nontension issue at all. So, of course, it's practically a foregone conclusion that, insofar as the sex problem is concerned, it's going no place."

Harold's method of trying to belong is to habitually use words that tend to intimidate the listeners into accepting whatever he's saying. The quasi-belonging words are, "It's generally understood that . . . ," "as you're well aware . . . ," "clearly, one would have to conclude . . . ," "naturally . . . ," "it's practically a foregone conclusion . . . ," and his favorite of them all, "of course. . . ."

The covert message is, "You can't reject what I'm saying because you'll be rejecting what 'you're well aware of' (unless you're a dummy). And you certainly must accept what is 'natural.' 'Of course' is the polite substitute for 'as any jackass can plainly see.' "

When Harold checks-in and decides to discard these semantic supporters, two things happen. First, his identity is turned on. Secondly, his pomposity is turned off. He takes full responsibility both for his words and for the ideas that these words represent. In no way does he use words designed to pressure others into accepting what he's saying. He is actual-belonging as follows:

"*I have an idea that the primary problem in sex education is that the right people aren't getting together. I believe that the schools offer sex education with the idea of reducing tension about sex among the students. And, at the same time, as I see it, moralists are interested in maintaining some tension about sex, since without this tension, morals may become looser. So I really think that the main disagreement has to do with tension versus nontension. The report from the president's commission, on the other hand, focuses more on rape and things like that without dealing with the tension versus nontension issue. So far as I can see, unless all these folks get together, the sex problem is going to get no place.*"

The most popular of the responsibility-reducers is *can't* or *couldn't*. The self-conditioning process here refers only to the inordinate or inappropriate use of these words. Following is an excerpt from a session of "can'ts." The student, Joe, is a psychologist and this is his third session:

JOE: *Somehow I just can't seem to find the time to be with the family. I'm so busy and I know Jill doesn't like it at all.*

DR. B.: *So you aren't with them very much.*

JOE: *No, not as much as I want to be.*

DR. B.: *Joe, would it be inaccurate to say you don't find time to be with them?*

JOE: *Don't—yeah, I don't. That's true. That's what I said.*

DR. B.: *I mean "don't" instead of "can't."*

JOE: *Don't—can't—that's okay with me. What's the difference?*

DR. B.: *"Can't is so absolute. It's finished, dead, done. The book is closed. "Don't" may be more accurate.*

JOE: *Yeah, I don't spend time with the family.*

DR. B.: *And when you say, "I don't," it's a more honest expression of yourself, isn't it? You're owning yourself now. You choose not to be with your family.*

JOE: *Uh, now—I—well, that's so. I choose not to. But sometimes I just can't. If it isn't something at the office, it's something at home that has to be done.*

DR. B.: *So sometimes you choose to be with them and sometimes you choose not to be with them.*

JOE: *Yeah, I'd have to say that.*

DR. B.: *You don't have to say that, Joe. You can say whatever you wish and use whatever words you want. You will anyway.*

JOE: *Well, it's hard to say, but it is true. Sometimes I choose not to be with them. Now, that's hard to say. Why do I say, "I can't be with them."*

DR. B.: *"Can't" implies that some external power other than yourself prevents you from being with them. I believe we all want to look good to ourselves and others, and sometimes I believe we pick up words and stick them where they don't belong in order to look good or not look bad.*

JOE: *But that's really—what you really look at it—it's a lie. I'm lying.*

DR. B.: *Not consciously, Joe. It's just a habit of communication that you learned someplace.*

JOE: (Becoming pensive, eyes on the floor)

DR. B.: *Where are you right now, Joe?*

JOE: *Oh, I'm just—it's nothing* (forced chuckle). *I say it's nothing and it is something. I'm just wondering why can't I just be myself and say it like it is.*

DR. B.: *Like you're doing right now? You're saying you can't be yourself and actually you are.*

JOE: *Huh? Oh, yeah—well, I mean I just want to be myself all the time.* (Sad tone)

DR. B.: *You're always being yourself, Joe—every second of your existence. You're being your sad self right now.*

JOE: *I don't get it.*

DR. B.: *"Be yourself" is a map without a territory. It's a hackneyed phrase that's meaningless. You're always being yourself. That's your power. When you're choosing to hide behind your "can'ts," that's you doing that, being your hiding self right then. When you're choosing not to hide behind your "can'ts," that's you being your more visible self. See how powerful you are?*

JOE: *Powerful? You mean when I'm being more—what did you say—visible, or honest, I'm being powerful? I don't get . . .* (trails off)

DR. B.: *Joe, your power is your awareness that you are pointing yourself in some direction from second to second—now-now-now-now-now-now.*

JOE: (Smiling with a self-pleased expression)

DR. B.: *What's tickling you right now?*

JOE: *I'm pointing myself in the direction that I "can't" be a psychiatrist, an M.D., because I'm a psychologist, a Ph.D. How about that?* (Smiling)

DR. B.: *How about what?*

JOE: *I used "can't."*

DR. B.: *True.*

JOE: *Well?*

DR. B.: *Well, what, Joe?*

JOE: *You said I shouldn't use "can'ts," so—so how can I be a psychiatrist today?* (Broad smile)

DR. B.: *I didn't say you shouldn't use "can'ts." It's true you can't be a psychiatrist today. I'm referring to the* inappropriate *use of "can'ts" or "couldn'ts," sticking them in places where they don't belong. Right now, when I check-out, I'm attending more to the nonverbal message you were sending—like, "I got you now."*

JOE: *Yeah—I thought I found a weak link in your chain.*

DR. B.: *And that's your power again, Joe—owning the satisfaction you may get in discovering a weak link in somebody's chain.*

126

JOE: (Sigh) *Yeah, I can do that. I do that with Jill when I put her down. I don't like that. That's something else.*

DR. B.: *And that's your power too—to not like to see yourself wanting to hurt your wife, or anyone. It's not that you* can't *stop trying to hurt her; it's that you* don't.

JOE: *Okay, it's getting clearer—this power thing and "can'ts."*

DR. B.: *Yes—the more you check-in and out, the more you become aware of your power, that it's really you that's moving you this way or that and you have choices.*

JOE: *I was—when you said "choices"—I use—I can choose—it's not whether it's right to use "can't" or not; it's that I always have the choice to use it or not.*

DR. B.: *Exactly. That's your power—and you make that choice all the time anyway. What's significant now, though, is that you are* acknowledging *that it's you who is the source of the choice. You're owning yourself, Joe.*

JOE: *Okay. I can't do this, I can't do that—that's me choosing to kid myself to—to save face.*

DR. B.: *And molding yourself in the process. Each time you use "can't"—this responsibility-reducer—it's easier to use it the next time. "I just can't get to places on time." "I can't get started in the morning." "I can't seem to stop getting traffic tickets." "I can't seem to stop drinking." "I can't stop blowing up at the children."*

My own experience and that of others in my group indicates that when an individual determines to limit or eliminate the inappropriate "can't" and "couldn't" from his vocabulary while clearly and honestly acknowledging responsibility for what he says and does, he feels pride in himself. He also senses gaining the respect of others without trying to manipulate others for this respect.

Semantic Strategies

Following, in brief descriptive form, are a few more of these unconscious semantic strategies that condition the way people think and feel. You may recognize some of them:

Conversation Bait: Leaving out the main idea of a statement. The person to whom he's speaking is now in the position of asking questions, like pulling taffy out of a machine, if he wants to get this main idea.

SARA: *Life is shitty.* (Slowing shaking head)

LYLE: *Why do you say that?*

SARA: *Oh, it just is. My father just called me.* (Grimaces)

LYLE: *What was it about—something wrong?*

SARA: (Dejected, exasperated tone) *Oh, he wants me to come up there, up north for a vacation.*

LYLE: *And you don't want to?*

SARA: *No, but the kids do.* [Etc.]

Another form of conversation bait is the dropping of a short declaration in the middle of a discussion. An example of this is, "There's another side to that, y'know."

This dangling lure can now hook the other person to ask, "What's that?"

A third variety of conversation bait is the lowering of the voice to an almost inaudible tone, inducing the other discussant to ask, "What?" or "I didn't quite hear that."

The usual conscious explanation that is given for using conversation bait is, "I feel that what I have to say isn't worth much" or "I feel afraid they won't want to hear what I have to say." The unconscious quasi-belonging aspect of this way of communicating is seen in the fact that the one practicing it chooses to drop the conversation bait into the discussion in the first place. The covert message is, "Prove your interest. Prove your acceptance of me. If you're really interested in me, you'll take my conversation bait and let me pull you in to me. I'm no longer responsible for what I'm saying because you're the one that's asking for it, not me. You can't reject me for doing what you're asking me to do." All of these remind me of the little boy who is holding his hands behind his back saying, "Guess what I got."

Overture to the Opera: Habitually introducing what he is going to say before saying it. "May I ask you a question?" "May I respond to that?" or "Would you like to hear what I have to say about that?" This preamble to the constitution is covertly saying, "Now hear this, hear this. I'm preparing you for something important and insuring your respectful, undivided attention to what I say, and therefore, to me. Also, you can't disapprove of anyone as polite as I am."

Disguised Question: Stating opinions in the form of questions—usually beginning with, "But don't you think that . . ." The nonverbal function of stating an opinion disguised as a question is to provide an aura of fair-mindedness. The quasi-belonging aspect here is the process of trying to persuade the other party to think as he thinks. The extra message is, "You can't really disapprove of my opinion or of me because I'm not actually stating it, I'm asking it."

The Hint: Habitually stating a position or making a request in the form of a hint, intimating or insinuating what he wants. "Stuffy in here, isn't it?" "I never know how you feel," or "I wonder if the baby needs changing." The quasi-belonging process here is, "If you pick up my hint and open a window, or tell me specifically how you feel about what I was saying, or if you get up and change the baby, then you are demonstrating both your understanding and your acceptance of me. But if you don't pick up the hint, then I can imagine that you're not really rejecting me because I never really specifically asked for anything in the first place. Perhaps you just didn't get it."

Prickly Pat: Choosing words that, while giving someone a verbal pat (compliment), adroitly inserts a prickly comment in the same sentence. "I like you so much better, Dave, when you're *open* as you are now, without your usual *varnish*." Extra message: "You can't disapprove of me and my little dig at you while I'm complimenting you."

Apologizer: Beginning or ending statements with, "Of course, this is just my opinion" or "That's just the way I see it" or "I'm sorry." The hidden message is, "You can't possibly reject or disapprove of anyone as humble and self-effacing as little ol' me."

I am convinced that the word habits mentioned in this chapter will tend to mold the individual in a *special* way. The habitual apologizer, through sheer repetition of the apologies, will tend to gradually diminish his self-esteem. The habitual snarler will move, with each snarl term, in the direction of a decreasing sensitivity for the feelings of others. The "should"-er will tend toward becoming a living machine, and those who habitually use "y'know" will become more and more dependent upon the reassurance of others for their own feeling of security.

Besides this *special* molding or conditioning of the individual by the words he habitually uses, there is also a *general* conditioning of the way he perceives, thinks, and feels. At the core of all of these communication habits there is an unconscious but still very real *misleading of both the listener and the self*. It is programmed *dishonesty* that is out of awareness. For example, when an individual uses these words, "I just *can't* stop blowing up at the kids," he is being dishonest both with himself and with the listener—only he doesn't know it. His more honest statement would be, "I choose to blow up at the kids." Also, like an old refrain running through all these word systems, there is a fundamental disowning of responsibility. What I'm suggesting here is that each time an individual uses any of these modes of communication he is unconsciously reinforcing dishonesty and irresponsibility in his person even though he may never consciously shirk a duty, steal a penny, or tell a lie.

You don't have to be imprisoned by your language. You're really free, at any time, to reshape your way of communicating. You can get into the habit of saying, "I am frustrating myself" or "I am having a temper tantrum" or "I am making myself self-conscious," whenever you choose to do any of these things. You can eliminate vaguerizers, responsibility-reducers, and other quasi-belonging syntax. You'll discover that your words will be molding you to be more honest and responsible toward yourself and others. You'll also discover that you are more respected by yourself and others.

7

Questions and Answers

THE FOLLOWING QUESTIONS AND ANSWERS WERE
compiled from two sources. Some were taken from a
large number of audio-and video-taped group sessions.
These are the questions most frequently asked by group
members. The second source was a meeting with
individuals who read the manuscript before publication.
Hopefully, this chapter will clarify some of the queries
the reader may have. There has been no editing of
these questions and answers except in the interest of
clarity.

Q. There's been so much written and said about love
    and being happy, and still, there are so many people
    who just aren't happy. It's hard to know what to
    believe.

A. It *is* hard to know what to believe. You can go to a church or Zen master or read a philosophical book and get different answers to the questions of life. You can then use this conflicting information to confuse yourself. We do know some basic facts, however. For instance, we know that we can learn more from experience than merely from lectures. A baby can learn a language in the first two years of life from experience without formal teaching. So it seems to me that, if you're seeking happiness, first on the agenda is not to confuse authority with truth. Don't confuse my authority with truth. Don't believe what I'm saying but rather, take from it what you wish and experience it for yourself.

Q. But what does happen to people to bring about so much unhappiness?

A. I believe that, for the most part, unhappiness is born, not from what is *happening* to the person. It's born more from what he is habitually doing, especially with respect to others.

Q. But if he's doing something that makes him unhappy, why doesn't he stop it?

A. That's the rub. He doesn't know he's doing it because it's so habitual. For example, he may be in the habit of manipulating others as a dominator or a seducer or a clinger or charmer and doesn't genuinely draw people to him, but it's out of his awareness. It's the only way he knows how to belong with others.

Q. He's still belonging in some way, isn't he? He does have some contact with other people.

A. Yes, and it's an illusion of belonging, not an actual-belonging. That's what I mean when I suggest that how happy he is has much to do with *how* he belongs with others, because *how* he belongs is what determines the feedback he gets from others.

Q. I wouldn't want to belong without a feeling of return. That would be empty. So how happy someone is must have something to do with selecting someone who loves him. Isn't that important?

A. Yes, that selection is important, but there is a chance factor involved also, being in the right place at the right time. Young people often marry without an awareness of the enduring qualities that make for a happy marriage.

Q. Are you saying that a good marriage, that selecting a mate, is just a matter of chance, of dumb luck?

A. Yes, to a large extent. Consider that of the hundreds of millions of available people in the world, the girl who is getting married may have no more than twenty or thirty people to choose from who happen to live in Long Beach at the same time she does and who happen to be single and who happen to be about the same age as she. Some girls have four or five fellows to select from. It can become less of a "selecting from" and more of a "settling for" this one or that one. I think that geography and chance have more to do with the selection than she does. If she happened to live in Alaska, she'd marry someone else.

Q.   You make it sound so dismal for that poor girl who is waiting for the right one who *just may happen* to be it.

A.   "It" will not "happen." "It" is a delusionary bridle path. She is not a "poor" girl. She is the *happener.* She's powerful, only she doesn't know it. She can make things happen. By checking-in and owning herself, she can develop a set of values that will attract certain human beings to her. By learning to check-out she can see others far more clearly and be better able to make a selection. Whatever belonging style she may develop, actual or quasi, she will attract certain individuals to her. Her belonging style can be like a flower to bees or garbage to flies. Instead of only thirty being attracted to this "poor" girl, there can be a hundred and thirty. And whether she chooses to have them attracted by her seductiveness or her being accepting of others is up to her.

Q.   All I'm saying is that what the reader wants is a *mutual* experience. Besides being accepting of others, he wants to be accepted by others.

A.   I believe most, if not all, of us want to be accepted by others, but before we can genuinely be accepted by others, we must be accepting of others.

And before we can be accepting of others, we must be accepting of ourselves. Before we can be accepting of ourselves we have to know just who this is we're accepting in the first place. We must know ourselves or, as I prefer to say, *own* ourselves, and that's where checking-in and checking-out come into the picture.

Q. The thing I'm wondering about is the person who, as you say, has behavior that is habitual. Say he's irritable and dominating and not getting a good feedback from other people, but doesn't know any other way of acting. At this point, when he checks-in and sees he's doing this for manipulative purposes, how is he going to find another way?

A. There isn't *another* way. I know this can be confusing. But this is more of an unlearning process than a learning one. When we're born, we have none of these habits that alienate us from others. We *learn* these habits, such as being irritable or dominating or fearful of others. These habits are like barnacles on our ship that we pick up from the sea of people around us. All we're doing is scraping off this barnacle or that one.

Q. All right. Take this person who is irritable and tense or dominating. What does he do to find another way, or, as you say, remove his barnacles? What's left then?

A. The magic words are, "He owns himself." He can check-in and catch himself in the act of being irritable and dominating. The moment he will take full accountability that it is he that makes himself irritable, that he *chooses* to be irritable and dominating, then and only then is he in a position to discard that habit.

Q. And then what's left? What does he have to put in its place?

A. There is nothing that he "puts in its place." Each of us is a composite of many qualities. He may have been an individual who was dominating, irritable, bright, and honest. Now what you have is a bright, honest person who is not dominating and irritable.

Q. Is that the time to check-in—when something negative is going on?

A. You can check-in anytime. When you check-out and discover that you're getting a poor feedback, perhaps even discord, from others, this can be a clue. It's a good time to check-in and honestly look at how you may be contributing to the discord. Listen to your tone of voice or any other way you're communicating.

Q. So that's the best time—when something negative is going on?

A. No. Check-in anytime. It isn't something you do at a special time. Preferably just creep up on yourself and discover if it's negative or positive. Often, Lill and I will check-in and say, "We're so lucky." It's fun to check into the positive and it becomes more than what it was before.

Q. Suppose you check-in and find some feeling like anger and you're not really sure if this is useful to you or destructive to you. Do you have a rule of thumb as a guide to tell you whether to discard this harmful emotion or what to do?

A. My rule of thumb is to own it. Be your own guide. If, when you check-out and check-in, you discover that you're cooperating in the hurting of someone or that you're lowering your own self-respect, you can discard it if you choose.

Q. Isn't there a time for anger?

A. Yes, also for tears. However, I believe that anger and tears are the two most overworked and powerful coercers of all. Of the two, I think that tearfully sitting on the pity-pot probably takes first prize and the temper tantrum, a close second. In my view, most anger is useless. It's a waste of time, but our language has arranged things so that we can indulge in anger at any time and not be responsible for it by saying, "He *made* me angry." Incidentally, I believe anger is a secondary process. First comes a feeling of fear, frustration or hurt. Then it's up to you as to what you do with that frustration or hurt. But your expression indicates I didn't answer your question satisfactorily.

Q. No. Are you suggesting I just bury my anger and pretend I'm not angry?

A. No, I'm suggesting that you can put your anger on the wash line and look at it, to check-in and own it as your own creation, your own habit. For example, imagine four women, all married to identical quadruplets. Each man has affectionate feelings but has learned the identical habit of being afraid to show his feelings of affection. The first wife has the habit of angering herself about this and elects to be vindictively sarcastic toward her husband. The second has the habit of depressing herself and crying about it. The third has the habit of making herself tense and fearful that he doesn't love her. And the fourth has the habit of dealing with it without trying to hurt or manipulate her husband but rather by encouraging him to become aware that it's safe to discuss anything with her. Each has her own habitual way of communicating. My suggestion is that each can own her own habit and then she's able to either keep it or leave it.

Q. I'd still like to know if there is such a thing as a rule of thumb to determine whether to accept anger when it does occur and decide this is how I'm belonging and this is acceptable in this particular situation, or whether at that moment to proceed to discard it.

A. A "rule of thumb" implies a "should"—some rule to go by, which can relieve you of the decision. You're a devoutly religious person, so let's consult the Bible for a rule as to whether or not to accept anger as a way of communicating. In Matthew *

---

* "Whosoever is angry with his brother without a cause shall be in danger of the judgment" (Matthew 5:22).

it says something to the effect, "Be not angry without a cause." Whoever heard of anyone being angry *without a cause?* When Tolstoi [10] encountered this curious phrase, he consulted the Tischendorf for the most ancient reading of the passage. He discovered that the words *without a cause* were nowhere to be found. They had been added by a fifth-century copyist. So if you want a rule of thumb as to whether you should be angry, you can use this biblical admonition, "Be not angry."

Q. But there are other passages in the Bible besides this one you're quoting.

A. Exactly. In Psalms * it says that God is angry with wicked people every day. In Ephesians † you are admonished to put *all* anger away from you, but also in Ephesians ‡ it says that you can be angry as long as you get over it before nightfall or before you go to sleep. I'm quoting these passages out of context and, for all I know, they might all mean the same thing, despite apparent contradictions. The point is that whatever the interpretation of whichever passage you choose as your rule of thumb, your integrity is intact as long as *you own yourself as the source* of that choice. This is another way of saying that your rule of thumb is inevitably you.

---

* "God is angry with the wicked every day" (Psalm 7:11).
† "Let all bitterness and wrath and anger and clamor and evil speaking be put away from you, with all malice: And be ye kind one to another" (Ephesians 4:31–32).

‡ "Be ye angry and sin not; let not the sun go down upon your wrath" (Ephesians 4:26).

Q. It still sounds like you're suggesting that I suppress myself, hold it in whenever I get angry.

A. No, I'm not suggesting that. I'm suggesting you look at what you're doing at the moment that you check-in, before your anger puts you on a yo-yo string. Generally, anger is a secondary process. Frustration, fear or hurt usually precedes it and each of these often involves being judgmental of someone or yourself. Then anger follows.

Q. I don't get your connection between being judgmental and getting angry.

A. Whenever you say something like, "That kid is so lazy, it makes me mad," the anger you experience is preceded by your being judgmental of the kid.

Q. So judge not lest ye be judged. That's your philosophy, isn't it?

A. No, that's not mine. I'm not suggesting you be non-judgmental out of fear of reprisal or retribution. All I'm saying is that I think it's a good habit to get into, being non-judgmental, because it results in a good feeling for everyone involved.

Q. When you say, "judgmental," you mean faultfinding, don't you? Finding fault with someone or yourself and putting that person down.

A. Right.

Q. Isn't that unrealistic though? Not ever being judgmental of anyone?

A. Yes, I'll agree with that, and it's also a time-saver.

Q. A time-saver?

A. Yes. I do believe that most things that we are judgmental about and get ourselves into a stew over are a waste of time, not to mention how illogical it is to be judgmental.

Q. Illogical? In what way? How can being judgmental be unrealistic and illogical at the same time?

A: I believe it's unrealistic to expect that you or I would never be judgmental or angry at anyone at anytime, especially if that person were close to us; but in most cases I still believe it is illogical.

Q. I really don't see what's illogical about being judgmental, finding fault with someone's behavior. There's a newscaster on TV who is the most pompous, flag-waving ass I've ever seen. I can't stand to even look at him anymore. I don't believe I'm looking at him illogically. He's simply a hypocritical, pompous ass.

A. You sound like you're making yourself angry just talking about him. Do you believe he could be any different at the time you saw and heard him?

Q. What?

A. I'm asking, do you believe he could possibly communicate any differently than he did, say, the last time you saw him?

Q. I don't know. That's how he communicates all the time.

A. Right. That's his way of belonging. He's the product of all the background of all his experiences, genetic, environmental, and cultural. He couldn't possibly be any other way at that very instant than the way he was. Perhaps the next instant, hour, week, year, or so, he could modify this pompousness if he knew he was pompous. But this is him right now, the sum total of all the experiences that preceded him. He doesn't sit up nights planning how to make you angry with him. He doesn't want you to not like him. It's his style of belonging. You can get angry with him if you wish but it's no compliment to you.

Q. But he thinks so black and white and superpatriotic and it's so obvious everything he does is for effect.

A. And the effect that he seeks is to be looked on favorably, but his way of going about it isn't satisfactory so far as you're concerned. That's all he can do right now, and the same is true for you. Your brain acts like a filter, and lets seep in only that part of the newscaster which will permit you to be judgmental of him. That's all you can do right now.

Q. You're saying I can't do anything other than be judgmental of that newscaster. Is that what you said?

A. Yes, at that moment. Perhaps the next moment or hour or week you'll choose to check-in and look at what you're doing, how you're thinking and choose to modify your thinking. But at that judgmental moment you're locked into the background of all your experiences which preceded that moment.

Q. I don't get what you mean when you called my brain a filtering device.

A. Okay. For the past few moments I've been thinking and telling you what I'm thinking. But you don't hear what I'm thinking. All you hear is what I say I'm thinking. You hear the symbols I use, called words, that represent my thoughts. But they don't represent the totality of my thoughts, only a tiny fraction of them. And when you hear these symbols or words which are feebly representing my ideas you filter only some of them in and block others out. And the ones you unconsciously filter in are only those that fit into the cubby hole of your unique set of genes plus the backlog of ideas you've been fed by your special environment and culture, which are all standing guard at the sentry posts of your brain. For example, if I were to say to you, "How do you like my new dog?" you will unconsciously pick and choose only a few elements of the totality of that particular "dog" and ignore the rest. It's in this sense your brain is like a filter. You filter in only those elements that your particular background of experiences will let you filter in.

   The same is true for how you feel, think, and communicate about that dog. If the dog is a beagle and you are a breeder of beagles you will filter in the size and shape of the dog, the length of its snout, the breadth of its paws. You will look at all of its dimensions. Another person who has been bitten by a dog will filter in the dimensions of the mouth of the dog and ignore other data. One who is allergic to dogs or fleas will automatically filter in the distance between the dog and himself. A hunter will filter in the relative effectiveness of the animal as a bird-dog. And for one who loves animals, he will filter in ideas of cuddliness. All these unique filterings arise from the symbol "dog," and each of the individuals, at that moment, can do no other. Each is locked into the background of all his previous experiences with mother, father, church, school, and he can filter in only what that background will permit him to filter in.

At another time, by checking-in and owning how he filters, he may opt to modify his filtering mechanism. In a sense he's becoming what he filters. So when you are being judgmental and angry at some person you really don't see him. What you see is only a puny fraction of him plus your unique way of belonging with that puny fraction which your background lets filter through. That's why I believe if you *really* want to be a more loving person you'll learn how to check-in and own how your filtering brain permits you to regard others right now and get out of your judgmental prison if you want. I'll say it again. You're continually becoming what you filter.

Q. Victor Hugo said that the supreme happiness is the conviction one is loved. Do you believe that?

A. That's a tough question—the "supreme" happiness—
if you had to choose only one—either self-respect
or being loved, which would you choose?

Q. Self-respect.

A. So would I. I know from personal experience
that it's possible to be very loved by many and still
not be happy because of loss of self-respect. So
Hugo could have said, "The supreme happiness is
the conviction one is loved and able to love others
and himself." I'd buy that.

Q. I think that it may be possible for very self-
conscious persons to try your technique and find
that they are more uncomfortable when they
check-in. They suddenly find out how very tight
they are all of the time and they are unhappy about
it. Should they check-out most of the time?

A. Yes, checking-out is especially important for
someone who has developed the habit of making
himself self-conscious. It's impossible to be
self-conscious and check-out at the same time. I
believe the reason for this is that you are outside of
yourself, looking and becoming more interested in
others rather than being inside feeling miserable.

Q. So you wouldn't recommend checking-in for
someone who is very self-conscious?

A. I would strongly recommend checking-in. However,
checking-in doesn't mean only looking at the "what"
you are doing, that is, being self-conscious.

Checking-in looks at the "how" you are making yourself miserable. What part of your body do you make particularly tight? What emotional sensation may be associated with this tightness? What do you tell yourself and believe? Will you own yourself as the architect of all this?

Q. I still have some reservations, though.

A. All right. Let's stop talking about things and have an experience.

Q. Right now?

A. Yes. We'll stop anytime you wish. Agreed?

Q. Okay.

A. Check-in this moment. What do you experience?

Q. I feel afraid, tight, very self-conscious.

A. Thank you. On a scale of one to ten, where ten is sheer panic and one is nothingness, total relaxation, where are you?

Q. Eight.

A. Check-in right now. Don't try to fight the fear. Let it be. When you fight it, you feed it. Look at it. Look at this so-called tightness or self-consciousness. Where can you experience it best? In your abdomen? In your neck? Where?

Q. In my stomach.

A. Good. Now give it a shape. Is it square, round?

Q. It's oval.

A. Good. Now, how large? Is it the size of an orange? A grapefruit?

Q. It's bigger than a grapefruit, like my whole stomach is filled with it.

A. Good. Now, on a scale of one to ten, where is this fear? Don't try to please me. Be honest with yourself.

Q. About five or six—that's interesting.

A. Yes, you're not fighting it now—just looking at it. Now, continue looking at this so-called fear. What is its source? What do you tell yourself to give it life?

Q. I tell myself people will look down on me. They'll really see me.

A. Good. Now check-out. Look at each one in the group. What do you see?

Q. Well, Dave is smiling like he's been through this before. And Mary looks—looks wide-eyed, fascinated. And John is looking at the rug. He looks—I'm wondering if he's scared like I was, and—

A. Right now—from one to ten—where are you?

Q. Two—three.

A. And your stomach?

Q. Comfortable. It's comfortable—pleasant.

A. Isn't that something. The moment you begin to look at yourself dispassionately, checking-in to what you're doing and how you're doing it, owning it—not fighting it, but owning it—your self-consciousness starts to dissipate. And when you check-out, get outside of yourself and really use your eyes, the self-consciousness almost disappears. You cannot check-out and be self-conscious at the same time.

Q. That's really—when I looked at John with his head lowered, looking at the rug—usually I would wonder if I'd done something wrong.

A. That's the whole point. Self-consciousness is, "What is he thinking *about me?*" Checking-out is, "What is he thinking?"

Q. It just occurred to me that I often feel like I'm controlling myself. Is this part of my self-consciousness?

A. Yes, excessive control is an old friend of self-consciousness. Where you find one you find the other. And curiously, the control-mad individual is really out of control. He's controlled, paradoxically, by the assumptive world he lives in. The assumption is, "If I express how I honestly feel or think, then all my inadequacies will show, or I'll look foolish, or you'll be hurt, or you won't like me." So he carefully guards most of what he says, often rehearsing it just before he says it.

Q. Yes, I'm aware I think like that. Is that a belonging style?

A. It's more of a habit that's found in lots of different belonging styles. But it is a habit that is associated with many other habits. For example, this excessive control works its way into the muscles, producing a tightness. Often there is minimal facial movement because the facial muscles have been instructed not to reveal too much—to be under control.

Q. What other habits go along with control?

A. I'm referring to *excessive, inordinate* control or restraint. The word is often used in our language as a wholly positive concept such as "He's well-controlled." But anything to excess isn't very positive.

Q. And what other habits accompany the habit of excessive control?

A. The control-mad one does little touching of others, especially in public. His assumptive fears control him. He rarely discusses his feelings, sometimes even with his wife. He embarrasses himself easily, is often an achiever, detail-conscious, duty-driven, and hobbles himself with one restraint after another until he has almost stifled his living in the now. It's as though he's lost control of his own free capacities for spontaneity.

Q. These habits you describe—I can see I've used a lot of them, but I didn't know it.

A. Yes. However, you let others know it continually even though you have no intention of doing so.

Q. I don't understand.

A. Most of the messages you send to others about yourself are unconscious. And most of the messages or responses you get from others are also unconscious.

Q. Now this is beginning to sound unreal, almost mystical. Do you mean that people have feelings and thoughts about me without my speaking to them?

A. Yes, you're continually sending out information about yourself to others without anyone knowing about it and they act upon it, too, without knowing they're doing it. I'll tell you of an experiment with some people that will make this clearer. Greenspoon [11] conducted a fascinating study with a large number of university students in this area of nonverbal communication. Each student was instructed to sit, one at a time, with the investigator and talk to him. That was his only instruction. He could talk about anything, but he had to continue talking. The investigator said nothing himself, but each time the student used a plural noun, such as cats, dogs, books, etc., the investigator would give a *negative* grunt. With each passing day of the experiment each of the students gradually *decreased* the number of plural nouns in his monologue. The fascinating aspect of the study is that when the students were invited to show how perceptive and sharp they were by explaining the meaning of the investigator's grunts, none of them could do so! Some said he grunted like that because "he didn't like what I was saying" or that the negative grunts were related to "mothers." Some guessed that the grunts were related to "females" or "males" or "being too assertive" or "being too unassertive" or too this or too that. None tied in the grunts with the plural nouns. The significant finding here is that the study demonstrated that people not only *receive* messages *unconsciously* but *act* on them *unconsciously*. And this is what I'm referring to. A person may be communicating nonverbally *without being aware that he is both sending messages to and receiving messages from the other*. Whatever your belonging style may be, that is, whatever you are giving, you are receiving minute by minute, consciously or unconsciously. If you tell yourself you're inadequate or adequate, worthless or worthwhile, fearful or fearless, interested in this person or disinterested in him, or anything at all—and you believe it —then that is true for you and you communicate that information constantly, second by second, without being aware of what you're doing, without saying a word. The message is picked up by the recipient, and he then can act upon the message in his special unconscious way of relating to you as though you are inadequate or disinterested in him, or whatever. Then, with this feedback from him, you can feel put down by the way he relates to you.

Q. That's a fascinating study. So how I feel about myself actually affects how others feel about me.

A. Exactly—but make the full circle. How you feel about yourself affects how others feel about you. They then send you messages that *also* affect you. You're literally constructing your own world from moment to moment, predicated on your belonging style. You reap what you sow.

Q. How am I constructing my world from moment to moment when someone else puts me down and makes me feel like an ass?

A. No one can put you down without your full cooperation. You construct your own world by whatever you tell yourself and believe at that moment, and how you choose to communicate at that moment. Eventually you come to see that while someone else may *try* to put you down, it's ultimately really you who puts you down. And if you stop putting yourself down, you'll discover that you don't need to be defensive.

Q. Are you suggesting that I not defend myself ever?

A. No, not if that someone is important to you and is falsely accusing you of something. I'm referring to the inordinate, ongoing defending of yourself to everyone and anyone.

Q. But how will anyone know where I really stand if I don't defend myself?

A. Everyone will know where you really stand whether you do or don't defend yourself. For example, when Mr. X checks-in, he discovers that he's told himself that he must defend himself with everyone at the drop of a criticism. He becomes aware that he has told himself (and believed it) that he can only find acceptance from others by immediately erasing each and every supposed noncomplimentary expression directed toward him. He tells himself (and believes it) that if he doesn't continually defend himself he'll be misread, misunderstood, and rejected. Thus, in *trying* to belong, his communicative system is filled with explanations, clarifications, and rationalizations in his desperate defense of himself.

Q. But isn't he straightening out the other person when he clarifies his position?

A. No, not really. That's the assumptive world he lives in. He may clarify a fact or two, but *he does not change the other person's view of him.* He succeeds only in reaffirming his insecurity in the minds of all who hear him. It's like trying to douse a fire with kerosene. Habitual defending of the self, including the words that are used, reinforces more habitual defending, until Mr. X is defending himself when he's never been accused of anything. That's why I like to say, "Power is defensivelessness."

Q. I don't quite understand when you say, "Power is defensivelessness." I don't understand where the power is.

A. Okay. Let's suppose Mr. X is really verbally attacked by another and he elects to return the attack with anger or defensiveness. He is at that moment, with his defensiveness, giving his attacker power over him. He is meeting violence with violence. However, if Mr. X chooses not to engage with his attacker in a defensive struggle, but decides instead to verbally check-out his attacker— that is, to withness listen to him, acknowledging in a friendly way his attacker's frustration and anger, in no way putting him down—Mr. X is manifesting his power at that time in a number of ways. He is turning away his adversary's wrath. He is gaining his adversary's respect for him. Above all, he is enhancing his own self-esteem and moving that much closer to actual-belonging, since he's learning, in a calmer place, just what the other is feeling.

Q. You said that everyone would know where I stand even if I don't defend myself. Suppose I'm Mr. X here; what would I be communicating if I didn't defend myself or try to get back at him somehow?

A. You're nonverbally communicating, "I acknowledge your frustration. You're choosing to try to hurt me with your judgmental words and I am *not* choosing to hurt you with judgmental words nor defend myself." That's all—nothing more.

Q. It sounds like you believe that people would be better off and there'd be more love if they'd stop being judgmental of each other. But that seems unrealistic to me. I think most people will stay the way they are the rest of their lives.

A.   I think it would take a lot of effort to stay the way you are now for the rest of your life. Our value systems are in a constant state of flux. You aren't the same person today you were a year ago. And you won't be the same person a year hence that you are right now. What we're doing right now is looking at the power we have to point ourselves in any direction we want.

Q.   Yes, I agree that our values change, but what I'm saying is that there are some people who, as long as I've known them, have been judgmental and gossipy and I believe they'll stay that way the rest of their lives.

A.   That's their belonging style right now, isn't it?

Q.   Belonging style? How can anyone belong that way?

A.   Not very well. That's why I coined the term "quasi-belonging." The extra message is, "I demand that you think and feel and behave in the way I want you to. Then you'll be acceptable to me and we'll get along fine."

Q.   Suppose, though, this individual is gossiping about someone who isn't there, really putting him down. How is he trying to belong there?

A.   The demand is still there: "Listen to what I perceive about this other person. See how perceptive I am. Listen to my disparagement of the other person. You can tell I don't like bad qualities like that and you can admire me for not being like that—and you better not be like that either. Admire me and be forewarned." Another quasi-belonging aspect here is the buddy-buddy process that occurs if the listener accepts the implied invitation to become a co-gossiper. Now together they can belong as mutual muckrakers, a sadistic quasi-belonging.

Q. I don't believe I'm very judgmental of others, but I sure put myself down a lot. Is that a belonging style, too?

A. Yes. When you put yourself down in a dialogue with someone, you'll notice, if you check-in and out, that you often evoke support and reassurance. The belonging system is, "I'm no good"—"Yes, you are." The quasi-belonging unwritten (and unconscious) contract is, "When I tear myself down, you build me up."

Q. And what if I put myself down when no one is around? What would you call that?

A. I'd call that one of the secrets of effective depression. We all have our special assets and limitations. However, the self-judgmental one arranges his misery by choosing to wallow in his limitations. By living in this quagmire he infects himself and everyone around him. It's as though he's put some strict parent on his back, grading everything he does, and the only grades he gives himself are D's and F's.

Q. Is that the main way that people depress themselves?

A. I don't know if it's the "main" way. Drinking alcohol is a large contributor to depression in our culture, since it is a central-nervous-system depressant. Here are five of the most common paths I've seen people follow to depress themselves.

1. Always try to exhort others to look upon you favorably. (They'll know what you're doing but try it anyway.)

2. Make lots of assumptions about lots of situations and be sure to treat these assumptions as though they are reality.

3. Then treat each new situation as though it's a crisis.

4. Live in the past and future only. (This means obsess about how much better things might have been and/or obsess about how terrible things might become.)

5. Occasionally stomp on yourself for being so stupid as to follow the first four in the first place.

Q. Okay. Now, what's a good method for dropping this habit of judging others and myself?

A. We are continually judging, that is, making judgments, making decisions. I'm using the word "judgmental" as "faultfinding." Practice checking-in and own yourself as the source of being judgmental, whether of yourself or others.

Q. You keep saying, "Own myself." I'm embarrassed to say this, but I'm not sure I understand what you mean.

A. Thank you. Will you check-in right now. What do you feel?

Q. Dumb—ashamed. (He appears crestfallen at this point.)

A. Good. Now, what do you tell yourself and believe?

Q. That they'll all, the whole group, will see how dumb I am.

A. Good. Now check-in further. What do you tell yourself about how the group will look at you?

Q. Well, they'll see how dumb I am—and look down on me.

A. Thank you. Are you dumber than George over there? [George is a psychiatrist who, moments before, called a member by the wrong name.] (*Laughter from all in the group at this point*)

Q. Oh, I'm not that dumb. At least I remember people's names. (*Much laughter in the group now*)

A. Now stop being so damn happy. You're supposed to be crestfallen and judgmental of yourself. I feel all mixed up. (*Laughter*)

Q. (*Still laughing*) How can I be crestfallen when you won't take me seriously?

A. Oh, it's my fault that you're not putting yourself down now. Incidentally, I do take you seriously, but I don't take your self-delusion that you're dumb seriously. Will you own all of this?

Q. I don't want to be like that. I'd like—there you go again. You say, "Will I own it," and I don't know what you mean.

A. Thank you. Do you feel dumb or embarrassed?

Q. No. I just feel like I want to understand.

A. Will you own, take full responsibility for wanting to understand, for not putting yourself down or being self-judgmental right now?

Q. Yes, and I don't want to be judgmental of myself. So when I own myself, that means I take full responsibility for what I'm doing?

A. Yes. For example, who wants you to be judgmental of yourself?

Q. What?

A. Who wants you to be judgmental of yourself? Is it some cosmic force?

Q   Well, no. I don't know.

A.   Is it me?

Q.   No.

A.   What's left?

Q.   Me.

A.   That's right. It's true you don't consciously do that, but you are the source, unconsciously, nevertheless. That's your power. Now, if you will own that, *truly* own that, you're now in a position to disown it. *But you cannot disown something you don't choose to own in the first place.*

Q.   One of the ways that I make myself miserable is by worrying that I might not get my vacation when I want it or that my speech won't go over. Is there anything else besides checking-in and out?

A.   Yes, there is. You can organize your worrying. Right now, when you worry, you do it any old time in a disorganized way. I'm suggesting that you continue worrying but do it in an organized way, that is, on the hour every hour for at least five minutes. This means that if you begin to worry at 6:30, you'll have to stop and wait until 7:00 before you can indulge yourself.

Q.   Are you kidding? I'm already worrying and you're telling me to continue doing it.

A. That's right. However, right now you're worrying on an unconscous basis and I'm suggesting you do it consciously, deliberately. This is given the name of *paradoxical intention* [12] and is a deconditioning process. You'll discover that it's difficult to do consciously something you've been in the habit of doing unconsciously. It really mixes those neurons up. Instead of the tail wagging the dog, now the dog will be wagging the tail.

Q. Well, I'll do it, but I'm afraid I don't see how it's going to work.

A. There's an old saying, "Fear knocked at the door. Faith answered and no one was there." Have some faith in yourself being able to follow the exercise, and the deconditioning process will take care of itself. The idea behind the process is that worry needs the future or the past in order to exist. "I'm afraid I said the wrong thing" (past) or "I hope this doesn't happen but it probably will" (future), etc. Now, you're going to be doing your worrying as an exercise, on command, at a specific time in the here and now. You're eliminating the future and the past. Be sure to select some top-notch worries, like you might suddenly lose bowel control and defecate in the middle of a board meeting, or five girls will mistake you for some rapist and take you to court—get something really worthwhile to worry about.

Q. You're making light of my worries.

A. Yes, a Zen master might say, "The truth of life is what's so and also so what." It's another way of saying, "Either you're going to make a big deal of everything or you're going to deal with everything." Either way you're going to have a considerable effect on yourself and everyone around you.

Q. You said that worrying needs the past or the future in order to keep it alive. That made a big impression on me. Do you think you live in the present all the time?

A. Oh, no. We need the future to plan and the past to learn from and reminisce. But living in the past or future continually is one of the secrets of eternal misery, a slow embalming process.

Q. I can feel pretty miserable when I think of the mistakes I made as a parent, especially with my son.

A. It's probably in everyone's interest if you look at the past as a place to learn from, the future as a place to grow toward, and the present as a place to live in fully. People who have learned to actual-belong spend most of their time in the present. Did you ever see two people who love each other gazing into each other's eyes? I've seen my daughter, Melody, and her husband, Steve, doing this. Their whole being is totally in the now. It's beautiful.

Q. That brings up the million-dollar question. What do you think love is?

A. Well, first of all, I don't think it's something that you wait to come to you. And it isn't something that you save up like money in the bank, waiting to invest it when the right one comes along. And I don't think it's an exclusive thing that pops up between two people and those two people only. I believe we're closer to the truth when we look at love as a continuum that expresses itself in a wide range of conduct, from the genuinely warm exchange between two friends to the glowing feeling we get when we look into the eyes of a certain special baby to the intimate experience of two lovers.

Q. I was thinking more about two people who feel that they're in love with each other and want to get married or live together. What is that love?

A. I've read lots of descriptions of love and almost all of them are filled to overflowing with flowery phrases. I used to please myself by writing some of these flowery phrases—things like, "When two people fall in love, then the energy created from this can melt the universe," and all that equinus manurus. I believe that if you really enjoy being with her and she with you more than anyone else, that's it. That's a part of love—that you're really comfortable together. I once told Lill, "I feel as comfortable with you as if I were alone." She laughed because it did sound funny, but she knew what I meant and appreciated it. The other thing that makes sense to me is that love is when the two people are bigger and better together than they were singly, a symbiotic relationship. And then there's that peculiar feeling, deep inside, like a gratitude to end all gratitudes, a floating feeling of euphoria—all these make up what I think of as love. That's all I know about it. You can add some of your own ideas to it.

Q. I think "respect" comes in there, too, don't you? I know lots of couples who don't seem to respect each other.

A. Yes. Sometimes couples aren't in love with each other as much as they're in love with the idealized image of how the other should be—and then they try to manipulate each other up to that image. I believe that unless there is a considerable respect for the dignity of each other, it isn't love. It's usually something else, and that something else is usually habituation to each other.

Q. And there's no hope for these people?

A. Sure there is. I believe anyone can learn to actual-belong if he chooses to do so. I don't hope people will grow when they set out to do so. I expect it. Growing means growing in all ways and it never stops. I know I love Lill now more than at any previous time and I believe this has a lot to do with the fact that I'm *in the now* more. I can see her more clearly now than before and also I'm more loving than before and that's something I learned from her.

Q. Something you learned from her—so you're saying we can learn to be more loving.

A. Yes. It's a never-ending thing. I think it begins from the day our mother first held us.

Q. You don't think heredity plays a part in how we're able to love?

A. Oh, yes, I do. That's why I like the word "belonging." It's an active verb and implies an ongoing "withness" for sheer survival. Without this predisposition to belong we'd perish—and I believe some have it more than others.

Q. You mean that some people may be born with more of a capacity to love than others?

A. I would say so—just like some are born with more muscular tissue than others. I've seen cats mothering their respective broods. One is always there, extremely protective and solicitous; and the other is gallivanting about. And I believe the same is true of human mothers.

Q. But that doesn't seem fair.

A. Well, it doesn't stop there. I think the genetic and environmental influences are intertwined. Anyone can take what he's been born with and develop it. If a person is born with just one finger on each hand, he can still learn to play the piano better than someone who won't study it.

Q. So we're back to learning.

A. Right. That's what it's all about—learning what our respective belonging styles are now and moving on from there.

Q. I'd still like to stay on love and marriage. What would you say are the absolute essential ingredients of a happy marriage?

A. Well, first of all, I think that if I could inject every couple with a hundred cc's of undiluted unselfishness, it would put a lot of us alleged mind doctors out of business. But whether in a happy marriage or a happy friendship, the ingredients are the same. Actual belonging is the harmonious music of honesty and responsibleness. Direct communication and "listening" are the instruments.

Q. What kind of honesty do you mean? Like not lying?

A. It's more like giving an honest feeling. And this honest feeling is like a pure gift with no manipulation involved. For example, "I really appreciate it when you . . ." They way I use "honesty" means that what you're feeling, thinking, and saying are going down the same track at the same time without any manipulation of the other intended. It's a refreshing experience if you're not accustomed to it. For example, in session with a fairly new group a few days ago, I had been talking about something—and I repeat myself occasionally—and when I checked-out right then,

I noticed that I was cooperating in the boredom of a few members. So I stopped and asked each to check-in at that instant. The first one said, "I'm going over in my mind what you just said," and the next said something similar and so did the next, and so on. And then this one girl said, "At the moment you asked me to check-in, I was and still am feeling a little apprehensive as to whether I put one or two eggs in the cake I put in the oven." I asked her if she was experiencing some boredom with what I was saying previously, nd she said, "A little bit, because I'd heard you say it before." The group spontaneously laughed at all of this, and when they checked-in again, they discovered that their laughter had to do with the honesty of the whole process. The honesty was like a refreshing dip in a cool brook. It's fun being honest.

Q. Yes, and it didn't sound like she wanted to hurt you.

A. Exactly. And that's another aspect of actual-belonging. She didn't volunteer, "You bore me!" with a snarl tone. I asked for it and she gave it to me but in a kind way. That's another habit of belonging. We can get into the habit of being direct and discreet simultaneously and choosing words that are true and not cruel.

Q. But even so, if I say something and it hurts someone, I feel responsible and you say that the other one is responsible for how he feels, responsible for hurting himself. I believe that if I were direct all the time, I'd have lots of enemies.

A. When I suggest that you can be direct and discreet, what I'm saying is that you don't walk up to some girl you've never met and say, "Pardon me, but did you know that you had one breast lower than the other?"

Q. But what I'm saying is that, even in a regular conversation, if I say something and I can see that what I said hurt this person, I feel responsible and guilty. What I hear you saying is that I'm not responsible, that each of us is the source of our own feelings.

A. You are responsible for *wanting* to hurt someone. If you could *absolutely predict* that your words would do that, as with a wife or a husband, then you would be entitled to some of the responsibility for that person's pain. But if you cannot do that, then you can't take full credit for that person's feelings of hurt. You're a *condition* for the feeling, not the source. For example, a shy person is often reluctant to look at someone when he's speaking to him. Now the person to whom the shy one is talking may misinterpret that the shy one doesn't like him and feel hurt. The shy one is responsible for *his* habit of lack of eye contact, and the hurt one is responsible for *his* misinterpretation and feelings of hurt. Is that clear?

Q. Yes, but if I really blow my stack and call someone a "phony" or something like that and they get angry, wouldn't you say that I started it, that I'm responsible?

A.   I'd say you're both responsible for cooperating in your discord. You're responsible for your feelings, your thoughts, and your words, and he's responsible for his. You're both the source and the cause of whatever you choose to have come out of your person. And when you condemn him like that, you're really condemning yourself, only you don't know it. Incidentally, I don't believe there is any such thing as a "phony."

Q.   You don't? Well, what do you call these people who pretend to be something they're not? There are lots of them on TV.

A.   I've never met anyone yet who considered himself "phony." It's a snarl term designed to cause pain. We all wear some kind of psychological clothing, and the psychological clothing of the so-called phony person is just a little more transparent than yours or mine. We all want the same thing—to belong. We've just learned different habits to achieve it. I feel the same way about all these labels—"radical," "leftist," "rightist," "pig," "neurotic." They're demeaning of the person who uses them and blind him from seeing the whole person to whom they're directed. I believe that the really tranquil one recognizes that he just does not have limitless energies and so he refuses to squander his energies on one judgmental thought after another, whether on himself or someone else.

Q. This makes so much sense to me. I know I could spend more of my energies appreciating myself instead of being so judgmental of myself.

A. Right, and you can even go one step further if you want. I do believe that one of the noblest pursuits of man is perceiving himself in the act of perceiving himself. For example, have you ever appreciated yourself in the act of appreciating something? If you've ever stayed in a cabin in the woods, can you appreciate the sound of a blue jay scolding you to come out and feed him?

Q. Yes, I've done that—and I do appreciate that.

A. Now, can you appreciate the fact that you have the capacity to appreciate that? There are some people who just don't appreciate that. They don't have that capacity. They have the capacity to appreciate other things but not that noisy blue jay. Do you see what I'm saying?

Q. Yes. I never thought of that—appreciating the fact that I can appreciate something. I can appreciate the fact that I can appreciate the artistry of some television commercial, that is, the photography, the setting, everything about it.

A. Yes, I know what you mean. I appreciate that also. And I feel lucky or grateful that I'm able to appreciate that. I often feel like saying "thank you" to someone for being able to appreciate so much. How do you feel right now? Where are you?

Q. I'm fascinated with this new idea. I feel great. And I appreciate the fact that I can appreciate you.

A. And that's actual-belonging. And you can appreciate the fact that you can see something to appreciate in almost everyone, if you check-out an selectively attend to that.

8
The Belonging Instinct*

RIVERS OF INK HAVE FLOODED US WITH THE
notion that animals are generally distinguished from
humans because the former behave instinctively and
the latter do not. But it doesn't seem reasonable to me
that nature would suddenly begin to run out of instincts
when she got around to humans. It would be more
characteristic of her to just add something—the ability to
think abstractly and create symbols of those thoughts.

* *Instinct* today is not a very popular term in scientific circles.
The term here refers simply to the existence of an observable
pattern of behavior that is not wholly explained in terms of
one of the "learning theories."

A short time after the mare drops the foal, the mare slowly ambles away and the foal follows. The mare doesn't take a walk at that precise time, at that precise gait, because it's a nice day for a walk, nor because she is acquainted with the physiological relationship between walking and increasing the foal's circulation. Nor does the foal follow because he reasons with his vast two-hour-old intellect that his milk wagon is leaving. They both behave in this precise manner at this precise time because, like grunion, they can do no other. Their inborn response systems are reciprocally activated. This means that the mare's instinctive ambling is activated by the foal's birth and that the foal's instinctive following is activated by the mare's ambling.

When the human mother moves, her baby also follows, first with the eyes, later on all fours, and still later by clinging to the apron strings.

A provocative study,[13] which furthers the consideration that humans may possess more inborn responses than we yet know, was conducted in a nursery for one-day-old babies. These infants were subjected to an extremely loud noise. They all reacted, but *how* they reacted was fascinating. Some of the babies cried, some extended their extremities, some flexed them, and some did very little of anything. When the experiment was repeated, the same babies responded the same way to the same stimulus. Thus, before environment or culture has had much, if any, influence on these human beings, they are demonstrating *inborn* responses to their environment.

A speculative step into the future might see the babies who extended their extremities also extending themselves to meet social stress, while those who flexed, that is, pulled in their extremities, might also pull in or withdraw from social stress. A replication of this study with five- and ten-year follow-ups should yield some interesting data.

Spitz [14] did a famous study which spotlighted the significance of human contact. This study was specifically concerned about babies in two different institutions. These institutions were different in a particular way. In the first, a home for unwed mothers, the mother or mother substitute took care of *two* babies, including holding. In the second institution for ninety-one babies, each mother substitute took care of *ten* babies. Thus the actual holding or contact was limited to diaper changing and bathing with little, if any, holding. Both institutions were rated as excellent in terms of hygienic, medicinal, and nutritional facilites.

The babies in the home with much body-to-body contact between the baby and mother figure developed physically and psychologically without impairment. The babies in the home with little body-to-body contact faired differently. I don't recall ever seeing a motion picture of babies that was more heart-rending than that of these babies. This was my first experience of looking at a full-screen exposure of the face of a baby conveying deep, hopeless, abject depression and sorrow. I never want to see that film again. The average mentality of all ninety-one had become that of a low-grade moron. In one of the groups, selected because of age (two and a half to four), only five of the twenty-one could walk by themselves and more than half couldn't even stand up. In this same group of twenty-one, the average number of words these children could speak was two. Six of them could not talk at all. Thirty-four of the ninety-one died.

Bowlby [15] has gone a step further. His research suggests that babies instinctively maintain contact with their mothers by means of not only their muscles (clinging) but also their facial expression and their vocal chords. He has postulated that babies come into the world with at least five *inborn* response systems, namely: clinging, following, crying, sucking, and smiling. Each of these instincts, activated at an appropriate time in development, tends to insure the baby's attachment to the mother and thus are essential for the *survival* of the baby.

When baby cries, Mother returns; when baby smiles, Mother stays, beguiled. (Did you ever try to walk away or not stay and smile when a baby smiles at you?) When baby clings, Mother holds; when baby sucks, the milk flows; and later, when baby is older and Mother moves, the baby follows. A further speculation is that the baby may not be the only one manifesting an inborn response system such as clinging—that the mother is also so governed, that when baby clings and Mother holds, *both* may be doing so because they can do no other, the clinging activating the holding and the holding activating the clinging.

This ethological hypothesis for human behavior is in contradistinction to Freud's [16] position, which states that the baby has a number of physiologic needs, such as food and warmth, but no *social needs,* that the baby recognizes the mother as a source of food and instinctively knows that losing the mother will result in the food no longer being available. Freud writes in *Female Sexuality* that "a child's first erotic object is the mother's breast which feeds him" and that by her care of his body, she becomes his first seducer. Thus, the basic position of psychoanalytic theory holds that the baby is driven to the breast because of its seeking to satisfy hunger and sexual instinctive needs. Ethologists reject this hypothesis, stating that there is no necessity in postulating a motivating force such as hunger or sex to explain the baby's sucking behavior, that the eye sees because it can do no other, and the baby sucks because its tongue, lips, and palate can do no other.

The thrust of the ethologist's position is that certain conditions in the environment or in the organism activate specific instinctual response systems in all animals, including human, that just as monkeys will become attached to a terry-cloth mother,[17] or ducklings attach to a human mother,[18] or a male stickleback fish will attach to anything resembling a pregnant female,[19] so a baby will attach to a nipple whether that nipple is connected to a breast, a bottle, or a rubber ring. Something curved, warm, flexible, moist, and nipple-like activates his lips and cheek muscles to respond by sucking. Secondary hunger satiation or sexual satisfaction thus can be seen as happy by-products, not the motivating force behind the response. Baby's sucking then is seen as a demonstration of a species-specific inborn response, which is another way of saying, "Babies are like that."

This ethological hypothesis for explaining some of human behavior appeals to me because of its refreshingly low level of inference, its high level of logic, and its availability to research. However, since the brain is the only thing that ever tried to analyze itself, and further, since I've painfully learned that for every complex, involved problem there is always a solution that is easy, simple, and wrong, I approach what I'm about to write with diffidence.

Bowlby has advanced the idea that when the instinctual response systems (crying, smiling, following, sucking, and clinging) are activated and the mother-figure is available, "attachment behavior" follows. What I am suggesting is that when a baby instinctively clings, and Mother instinctively holds, a new or secondary *instinct of belonging* is permanently activated in that baby. *This belonging instinct includes any behavior that involves seeking acceptance, approval, esteem, or love from others. And it is manifested in his facial or body movements, his thoughts, his feelings, and his mode of communication, from moment to moment for the rest of his life.*

I prefer the term *belonging* to Bowlby's "attachment behavior" appellation or Lorenz's "bonding" because *belonging* hopefully incorporates the idea of a concomitant emotional state that is reinforcing the experience of belonging. This secondary response, *belonging,* can remain a latent or potential instinct, forever dormant unless activated by the baby's clinging, crying, etc., but once activated, I believe it becomes the *dominant instinct* in human behavior, and is manifested in *every* human contact.

Comparative ethologists point out that instinctive response systems are accompanied by emotional states peculiar to each. There is an emotional response accompanying smiling, another attached to crying, another to sucking, etc. I would like to add that these response-emotional states are not constant. One may smile with a feeling of amusement, derision, joy, tension, or pride. One may cry with a feeling of sadness, gladness, anxiety, relief, or pain. The emotional response attached to belonging, in contrast, is consistently experienced as a feeling of *well-being.* In this sense you can perceive yourself as experiencing varying intensities of belonging at any given moment with any given individual measured by the relative state of well-being that you feel at that moment. It becomes clear that any "belonging duo" can experience varying degrees of belonging ranging from the ritual handshake, with its mild satisfaction of ostensible acceptance, to being in love, with its energizing sensation of euphoria.

This instinctive need for direct, physical, sensory contact doesn't stop with babies. Whatever the age, we still need it. As we grow up, this innate need to make contact, to belong, can be observed in verbal and social form as well. And sometimes we can seek to belong in more abstract ways. We can belong to a flag, a deity, or a duty, and these can serve as the substitute *other* that, in infancy, was the mother.

One last conjecture is that in later periods of life other instinctual response systems are activated which may be an integration of a number of earlier instinctual responses that are influenced by the culture and environment. Some of these may include (1) defending behavior (defending one's self, one's family, one's territory); (2) empathic behavior (experiencing sorrow or gladness for the pain or pleasure of another); (3) courting behavior; (4) heterosexual behavior; (5) hierarchy behavior (sensing one's esteem ranking—that is, self-esteem—called "pecking order" in the animal world).

I'll stop now with all these speculations regarding instinctual responses that may bloom later in life. My interest here lies in directing your attention to the ingredient common to all, in that all can be conceptualized in terms of *belonging*. My position is that if the survival instinct is the king of instincts, then "belonging" instinct is the queen, superseding all other inborn responses, including sex and hunger.

I'd like to make a parting remark on babies and parents that may bear on the psychological health of both. I believe most of us can recollect holding infants in our arms. As you recall, some of them are born like wriggly worms. You feel as though you've achieved a truce, that he's in a relaxing position, and then you discover that he's just been relaxing between rounds. With one strategic move of his little, deft, and devious arm, he has broken all the rules of fair wrestling and has a mini half nelson on your tie and eyeglasses simultaneously. On the other hand, you can probably also recall holding little "angels," so quiet, placid, and content. In fact, these little babies are referred to as "born angels," possibly implying that the wriggler is not so good. Now, if a mother who is attracted to wriggly babies *gets* a wriggly baby, then the belonging experience is off and running. But if a mother who has a preference for placid babies gets a wriggly one, then some recycling of her thinking habits is indicated, lest she nonverbally communicate her dissatisfaction to her baby.

I wanted to spend some time on this idea because I believe that babies and young children are exquisitely sensitive to the silent message, the facial expression, or the tone of voice—much more so than adults. They can be seen as closer to animal life than human life in that the first two years of their lives are spent in receiving nonverbal cues, feelings, and vibrations from others. My conviction is that when a baby is held, he is informed through this animal sensitivity just how the holder feels about him, that is, whether the holder is resentful or is doing a "duty" or enjoys holding. If what I've just said is true, then so-called neurosis can begin from day one. In any event, I invite mothers and fathers to check-in and examine their feelings, which they may be unconsciously broadcasting to their babies. Be clear on this. The mother may feel resentful toward her husband. If she sits down and holds her baby to feed him at that precise moment, the likelihood is that that feeling tone will be picked up by the baby. The baby doesn't reason out whom those angry feelings may really be directed toward. He just receives them. So check-in before feeding or holding your baby. Even have some nice pleasant music playing at feeding time. Who knows? You may prevent an ulcer later on—for both of you.

9
Summary

Quasi-Belonging Is an Internal Struggle

This incessant battle is waged between the style that proclaims, "I'm super-self-sufficient; I don't need you" and the deeper, actual self that avows, "I'm not truly all that self-sufficient. I really do need you. I want your acceptance but I'm afraid to risk your rejection." If you quasi-belong, you can recognize this internal struggle. It takes the form of heightened tension whether you are with a group of friends or strangers.

Actual-Belonging Is an Inner Peace

The energies of this process send the singular message, "I'm neither above nor below you. I'm with you. I know you wish my acceptance as I wish yours, and I am content not to persuade you toward that end." There is no struggle here—just an inner peace.

Following is a compendium of the principles crucial to actual-belonging.

ACTUAL-BELONGING BEGINS WHEN:

I totally own how I think and feel, and how I communicate these thoughts and feelings.

I choose not to puppeterize you for your approval of me.

I practice withness listening until I understand what you understand and feel what you feel.

My communication to you is clean, clear, and congruent—my feelings, my experience, my words being one.

I rid my language of "labeling" words (snob, crybaby, neurotic, phony, stupid), which blind my seeing the whole human being so labeled.

I acknowledge the power of my defensivelessness. I choose not to lean on the borrowed staff of others.

I neither communicate nor behave with chronic indecisiveness or helplessness.

I acknowledge that whatever I tell myself and believe is then true for me, and I live accordingly.

ACTUAL-BELONGING IS NOURISHED WHEN:

I neither spread the germs of gossip nor encourage others to do so. I let the talebearer see there is excitement to be experienced at the expense of no one.

I acknowledge that I am not entitled to guilt unless I have deliberately or thoughtlessly caused hurt or possible future hurt to others or myself.

I can see a sea of unrepeated faces and acknowledge that, for every face, there's an unrepeated, unique way of thinking and feeling.

I don't make a big deal of everything. I deal with everything.

I condemn not a single soul. In condemning him I condemn myself. In accepting his difference, I accept my own.

I don't look at the world through dark-colored glasses or through rose-colored glasses but through clear glasses and accept what I see.

I can look for some beauty in every soul.

The following principles are presented in terms of the *inner peace* that flows from and permeates every element of *actual-belonging*. I would like you to see how synonymical and interchangeable these two concepts are:

INNER PEACE MEANS:

I believe I am, minute by minute, harvesting what I seed in my thoughts, my feelings, and my words. When I seed acceptance of others, I am harvesting acceptance of myself and acceptance by others simultaneously.

Whether I am with a rose, a kitten, or a human, at that moment in time that rose, that kitten, that human, is the center of my world.

Not trying to be humble but being humble, acknowledging that an excellent medicine is taking myself with a grain of salt.

I can experience the real joy of another's real joy and the real grief of another's real grief.

I am not imprisoned by my language.

I can see each human as infinite—always able to move toward his potential, whether he's eight or eighty.

My feelings are my gift to you and I demand nothing in return. My feelings are not expressed to sway you.

I acknowledge that how I communciate is like the ripple on a pond, affecting all in my sphere of contact and returning from shore to affect me.

Seeing my anger as a corroding indulgence of my brief stay here.

I see everyone as wanting to belong, no matter what his words. I hear his words. I listen to his want.

I am grateful for our moment together.

Asking myself, "Am I true? Am I true?" and hearing my own unequivocal response, "You are, you are." Inner peace is the feeling of joy when I hear that response.

THE BEGINNING

INNER PEACE IS
SEEING THE PAST AS
A PLACE TO LEARN FROM,

THE FUTURE AS
A PLACE TO GROW TOWARD,

AND THE PRESENT AS
A PLACE TO LIVE IN FULLY.

REFERENCES

1. Albert Mehrabian, *Silent Messages*. Belmont, Calif., Wadsworth Publishing Company, 1971.

2. Best, Coe, Moore, Read, Clay, "Irradiation of the Pituitary Gland in Hypertensive Vascular Disease," *American Journal of Medical Science*, 1950, p. 276.

3. Steward Wolf, "Effects of Suggestion and Conditioning on the Action of Chemical Agents in Human Subjects," *Journal of Clinical Investigation*, 1950, p. 100.

4. W. B. Connon, "Voodoo Death," *American Anthropology*, 44: 1942, p. 169.

5. Silvano Arieti, "Voodoo Death." *American Handbook of Psychiatry*, 1959, pp. 558–59.

6. B. B. Gorton, "The Physiology of Hypnosis," *Psychiatric Quarterly*, 23: pp. 317–43.

7. A. M. Weitzenhoffer, *Hypnotism*. New York: John Wiley & Sons, Inc., 1953.

8. Alfred Korzybski, *Science and Sanity*. New York: Science Press Printing Company, 1933.

9. S. I. Hayakawa, *Language in Thought and Action*. New York: Harcourt, Brace & Company, Inc., 1941.

10. Lyof N. Tolstoi, *My Confession, My Religion, the Gospel in Brief*. New York: Thomas Y. Crowell Co., 1899.

11. J. Greenspoon, "The Reinforcing Effect of Two Spoken Sounds on Frequency of Two Responses," *American Journal of Psychology*, Vol. 68, 1955, pp. 409–16.

12. V. E. Frankl, "Paradoxical Intention: A Logotherapeutic Technique," *American Journal of Psychotherapy*, 14: 1960, p. 820.

13. M. D. Fries and P. J. Woolf, "Some Hypotheses on the Role of the Congenital Activity Type in Personality Development," *The Psychoanalytic Study of the Child*, Vol. 8, New York: International Universities Press, 1953.

14. R. Spitz, "Hospitalism, an Inquiry into the Genesis of Psychiatric Conditions in Early Childhood," *The Psychoanalytic Study of the Child*, Vol. 1. New York: International Universities Press, 1945, pp. 255–78.

15. J. Bowlby, "The Nature of the Child's Tie to His Mother," *International Journal of Psychoanalysis*, Vol. 39, 1958, p. 350.

16. S. Freud, *Three Essays of the Theory of Sexuality*, Standard ed., Vol. 7. London: Hogarth Press, Ltd., 1953, pp. 123–245.

17. H. F. Harlow, "The Nature of Love," *American Psychologist*, Vol. 13, 1958, pp. 673–85.

18. K. Lorenz, *King Solomon's Ring*, New York: Thomas Y. Crowell Co., 1952.

19. N. Tinbergen, "An Objectivistic Study of the Innate Behavior of Animals," *Biblioth. biotheor.*, Vol. 1, 1942, pp. 39–98.

Index